Marriage

vs.

Ministry

The Fight of My Life

Orienthia Speakman

International Standard Book Number 13: 978-1948731201
Cover Design by Dream Design Graphics

Editing provided by Publish*her* Publishing

www.publishher.org

DEDICATION

To my best friend, partner, husband, and my chocolate drop:

I thank God for allowing us to go through this trauma in our marriage in order for us to get to this place, a place of confidence and assurance that what God put together, let no man tear asunder, not even us! I thank God every day for blessing me to wake up to you by my side. I thank Him for allowing us to experience brokenness in our relationship because that same brokenness is blessing us and others.

I am now a better wife, a better mother, a better person because of the wisdom of God that I learned during our restoration. Vincent, you are such an amazing husband, and I honor you! I smile sometimes when you're not even aware because your father's traits and characteristics are very present through you. You have been an awesome father to all five of our children, and I am so thankful.

Our love is not perfect but it's pure. God saw that and granted us this opportunity to make it last forever! I plan to do just that! I love you honey.

Happy 8th year Anniversary!

Love Always,

Your Caramel Princess

CONTENTS

FORWARD

We are honored to have the opportunity to write the forward to our spiritual daughter's second published book. We want the readers to take time and investigate Pastor Orienthia's life through this awesome testimony of restoration in her marriage. We pray you are blessed, encouraged, and empowered d as we were. This book is not a prettied-up version of marriage and ministry, but it deals with the devastation of what happens when the two are unbalanced.

Pastor Orienthia Speakman, the wife, mother, friend, daughter, coworker, and Woman of God, shows you her own personal story of how God took her broken marriage and made it whole. She opens her life, chapter by chapter, to help married couples understand the route of brokenness and restoration that she and Vincent endured. As their counselors, we witnessed the pages of this book up close and personal. We are proud to say that this couple was willing to do the work that was needed to see the purposes of God begin to build their marriage His way.

Papa Nick and I have always viewed Orienthia as a rare jewel from the very beginning, a woman filled with life and a quest to live it on purpose. She is strong, courageous, and full of tenacity. This is one of the reasons why the enemy could not defeat her. She walks in the power of God and expresses love on all levels. Her strength stood out as I watched her endure things that would have overthrown others, but she remained steadfast like Joseph. She desired to have a marriage that reflected The Word of God, and she was willing to fight every step of the way.

She has a special love for women and marriage. She truly desires to see couples living their best married life. This book will become a tool, full of practicality to assist those that are married and in ministry on how to defeat the enemy and his devices that are set up to destroy your union. You will see in this book how marriage and ministry go hand in hand, but there must be an order to it all, and God must be front and center.

Our spiritual daughter is truly a Proverbs 31 woman, not because she's been perfect, but because she has made some mistakes ALONG THE WAY AND turned them into triumphs. We love you, daughter, so much, and thank you for giving of yourself so freely to the body of Christ. We are extremely proud of you and the work you've done on this project. It is phenomenal!

"Just as by melting two candles together you get one piece of wax, so, I think one who receives the flesh and blood of Jesus is fused together with him, and the soul finds that he is in Christ and Christ is in him" ST. CYRIL OF JERUSALEM

"Just as the Eucharist makes us one with Christ, a good marriage makes us one with each other."

Nicholas Simpson Sr.

Pastors Nicholas & Carol Simpson (aka Papa Nick & Momma Carol)

Shekinah Glory Ministries Las Vegas, Nevada

www.shekinahglorylv.org

ACKNOWLEDGEMENTS

Father (God), Son (Jesus), Holy Spirit (Guide):

I first and foremost dedicate this book to you because without you, it wouldn't have been possible, nor would it have been completed. Thank you for guiding my thoughts and my hands through this project. May it bless every reader.

Rev. Nicholas & Carol Simpson and The SGM Family:

Thank you all for your love, support, and prayers. Thank you as a church for accepting us and allowing us to minister to you when we are in Las Vegas! Momma and Papa Nick, thank you for not only setting an example, but for taking Vincent and I under your wings while our marriage was broken. Thank you for nurturing us back to a healthy place in our marriage and for living what you preach and teach! We are so blessed to have you both as our spiritual covering. We are honored.

My Father, Rev. Eddie Dorsey:

Rest in heaven, Dad! I just wanted you to know I'm doing what I promised. Preaching, writing, giving God my best, and I'm happily married. Your deposits of wisdom keep me going. Every prophetic word that you gave me on that couch is coming to past! Love you forever, dad!

My Mom and Step-father (Marilyn and Ernest Williams):

Every storm has an expiration date! Thank you both for always praying and encouraging us through ours. Thank you both for cheering us on and for never judging us. Mom, you are always by my side, and I am forever grateful.

Idella McIntyre & PublishHer:

Thank you for coaching me through this project and for being a loyal friend. Not only did you pray for us, but you gave me spiritual wisdom that counteracted and shook every devil that was coming for my marriage. PublishHer was my Elizabeth and my midwife. Not only did it make my book leap on the inside through creative development, it also helped me birth it into existence. I loved the hands-on approach and author support your services provided. Your excellence is greatly appreciated.

Our Children:

Being a blended family is awesome! Each of you made the restoring and repairing of our marriage easy. Vincent Jr, Quovadia, Ebony, Alexcia, and Joshua, thank you all for being in our corner.

Rodney Billings Sr.:

Rest in heaven, man of God. Your words to me were a healing balm to my soul. Many didn't even see the pain I was in that Sunday from the brokenness of my marriage, but God sent you with an encouraging word.

I had lost hope. God used you to help me hold on. Thank you for your kindness. I never forgot.

Our Siblings:

Thank all of you for your support, whether it was through helping me move (out or back home) or speaking truth to Vincent and me. We know in our hearts you all wanted us back together. God answered your prayers.

Friends and Ministry Partners:

Thank you! With tears in my eyes, to know that people genuinely love you and care in your time of trouble is priceless. I couldn't write all the names because there was so many that reached out, got in our business, came from your city and state to check on us and gave encouragement and hard truth. Thank you! Some of you even opened up your churches and ministries and have allowed us to share our testimony. You all are a blessing to our lives. You saw past our ugly separation and assisted us in our restoration. Vincent and I are forever grateful.

Readers and Ministry Supporters:

My prayer is that this body of work will be a blessing to your life. My hope is that deliverance, wisdom, restoration and peace will be present on each page. I declare breakthrough in your marriage and or life as you have sown into ours. Thank you in advance. Our marriage has been exposed that others may be encouraged, educated, enlightened, and restored in Jesus name!

1

THE FIGHT OF MY LIFE

Marriage versus Ministry. Who, in their right mind, would ever think this would be a battle? Why would this have ever been a struggle in my relationship? I'm a Christian woman who has the call of God on me, and I am a wife to a man whom I love very much! Out of all the issues and challenges in life, these two are on opposite sides of the ring. In my mind, many times, it has played out in my head like a boxing match! Instead of coming into the center of the ring to agree or work together, both entities seem to have been in their corners, waiting for the bell to ring so they can come out swinging—only to see which area was going to get knocked down and counted out! It seems as if God is forcing me to choose, but how can that be correct when He created both?

There are silent wars that go on behind closed doors. Many couples are in a boxing match in the spirit that's causing devastation to our relationships, the unspoken subjects that aren't touched because we as ministers don't want people in our business as it pertains to our marital struggles. I discovered this to be factual as I was posting on social media about my marriage. I'm going to write it just like I posted it on Facebook. I'm warning you because my grammar is not always correct and most times on purpose.

COUNT DOWN TO MY ANNIVERSARY... 5 MORE DAYS

#ThingsIveLearned (whew this one gonna hurt)

When my marriage fell apart and divorce papers were on the table (yep) I blamed my husband for everything. In my mind, it was all his fault because I was walking out the call of God on my life. It wasn't until God showed me that the mistress/manstress (a word I made up since when women cheat we don't use mistress) in my house or the side piece in my house was MINISTRY. I'm not speaking about my relationship with God but all my outside activity that I had allowed to be my priority instead of my marriage. I was having an affair with my prayer lines, my speaking engagements, and my book writing which cause me to neglect him. I had become a public success but a private failure. This pic was the night God broke me and the road to recovery began. I stopped praying to God to fix him. That day my prayer was Lord work on me! I'm the problem... yes, he has issues but God, FIX ME! Real maturity is when you can look past the faults of your spouse and see YOURSELF!

Here's the order ladies:

1. GOD= your personal relationship with Him

2. Husband= Your first Priority

3. Family= Children, parents, friends, etc.

4. Ministry= Your activities for church, speaking engagements, book writing, prayer lines etc.

I thank God for delivering me so that my marriage could heal. God was working on him as well but that wasn't my business. I needed deliverance from myself and I am so much better for it.

That post received over 500 likes, but what was more shocking was the inboxes and emails that followed. I was receiving emails from Pastors' wives and from women who were in ministry and were married to men who were not. I even received a few messages from men who felt their wives needed a class on how to put them first. Both ends of this spectrum were hurting, and these individuals were genuinely looking for help. I had been tricked by the enemy in thinking that I was the only one in the world who would have a problem like this! It turns out, I wasn't alone.

On the day I made that Facebook post, my marriage had been exposed through the revelation that it had taken a major hit from the tricks of the enemy. The devil's goal, of course, was to destroy my marriage, but even after being knocked down, we got back up for another round! The opponent of all marriages is the devil and his devices. His desire is destroying the family unit, and he does that by trying to destroy our relationships. Every fighter must have a tactic or strategy to win because no boxer enters the ring with the intent of losing, especially to a knock out!

Boxing is a combat sport in which two people, usually wearing protective gloves, throw punches at each other for a predetermined set of time in a boxing ring. Each opponent's goal is to win—either by knocking his opponent out, which means one opponent has been hit so hard and/or so much they are unable to continue the fight, or the winner is pronounced based on the judges' score cards at the end of the contest. There are times when both fighters gain equal scores from the judges. In such cases, the fight is considered a draw or a tie between the two fighters.

The matches between fighters are usually overseen by a referee to ensure all rules are obeyed. Since boxing is a contact sport, there are usually injuries that occur. Before rules, regulations, and weight classes, fighters would fight to the death or until one opponent surrendered. The surrendering usually occurred because that fighter couldn't take another hit.

Don't be surprised when I say this, but your marriage will take some hard hits in the ring. As a matter of fact, you're probably reading this as a source of encouragement because you've already been hit! And to those of you whose marriage is like mine, where one partner is actively called to a level of ministry, it seems the hits are harder and sometimes unfair, even with our

Referee, God, present. I call God the "Referee" because He oversees every situation in our lives before we go through them. I love the Scripture:

"In Him also we have received an inheritance [a destiny— we were claimed by God as His own], having been predestined (chosen, appointed beforehand) according to the purpose of Him who works everything in agreement with the counsel and design of His will," Eph 1:11 (AMP)

This assures me that God as my Referee will make sure the enemy adheres to the rules of the fight, but also, God is with me to ensure that I win! It's not really a fair fight because my victory has already been declared over the enemy. That doesn't mean I won't get hit hard, but it does mean I won't be counted out nor knocked out without being able to get back up! I use boxing terminology because, even as a girl, I found it a fascinating sport to watch!

Vincent and I viewed marriage and ministry as two separate entities in our relationship; therefore, it was always a battle. It seemed as if he represented the marriage and I represented the ministry, which caused us to always go toe to toe. We became each other's opponent instead of being on the same team. We didn't realize that we both were wrong because the real enemy was our selfishness towards each other and wrong perspectives with how to balance our marriage.

While other couples may be on opposite ends of the ring in finances, whether it's time to start having children, chores, or work, we were fighting about how much ministry I was doing! Yes, ministry had become a hot topic in my home and not in a positive manner. My husband never out right said that this was his issue, but his attitude every time I mentioned doing another workshop, flying to another state to speak, or going to an extra conference just made him more distant. His distance made me feel unsupported, and then we landed in a very dry and barren season in our marriage that almost destroyed it.

More details are in the upcoming chapters concerning our other issues that were resolved, but I want to be very candid with ministry leaders for a moment. NEGLECTING YOUR SPOUSE, YOUR MARRIAGE, YOUR HOME, YOUR FAMILY, IS NOT THE WILL OR HEART OF GOD! YOUR FIRST MINISTRY IS YOUR HOME! I realize now, after it almost destroyed my relationship, that my perspective of ministry and marriage being separate was incorrect. I felt that my ministry work was priority because I was saving lives, blessing other families, healing the broken spirited, and laying hands on the sick. I felt that running to the hospitals, being at all the services, or coaching and counseling those that needed me was my way of pleasing the Lord. MY perspective was blinding because I didn't see that I was neglecting my home, but more importantly, my husband.

In my mind, I would tell myself that my husband was already saved and that he knew he married a preacher. We had this discussion in counseling, so why is this a problem for him now? Many of you tell yourselves that same lie while your spouse and family are starving for your attention and affection. I am not here to judge your relationship, but I am hoping that this is a resource to bring conviction and order to the body of Christ in this area. Since I am a female, I want to tug at my sisters' heart strings about being sure we stay in the order of God in this area of marriage and ministry. The Bible, of course, does address the qualifications of a leader, including the fact that he should be able to manage his own family first. Ladies, this doesn't exclude us. As a matter of fact, since I'm the preacher in my household and my husband is not, I plugged myself right into this Scripture that is found in I Timothy 3:1-13.

Qualifications for Overseers and Deacons

3 Here is a trustworthy saying: Whoever aspires to be an overseer desires a noble task. ² Now the overseer is to be above reproach, faithful to his wife, temperate, self controlled, respectable, hospitable, able to teach, ³ not given to drunkenness, not violent but gentle, not quarrelsome, not a lover of money. ⁴ He must manage his own family well and see that his children obey him, and he must do so in a manner worthy of full respect. ⁵ (If anyone does not know how to manage his own family, how can he take care of God's church?) ⁶ He must not be a recent convert, or he may become conceited and fall under the same judgment as the devil. ⁷ He must also have a good reputation with outsiders, so that he will not fall into disgrace and into the devil's trap.

⁸ In the same way, deacons are to be worthy of respect, sincere, not indulging in much wine, and not pursuing dishonest gain. ⁹ They must keep hold of the deep truths of the faith with a clear conscience. ¹⁰ They must first be

tested; and then if there is nothing against them, let them serve as deacons. [11] *In the same way, the women are to be worthy of respect, not malicious talkers but temperate and trustworthy in everything.* [12] *A deacon must be faithful to his wife and must manage his children and his household well.* [13] *Those who have served well gain an excellent standing and great assurance in their faith in Christ Jesus. 1 Tim 3:1-13 (NIV)*

I was in violation of the Word of God because my marriage was falling apart while I was ministering to the masses. It wasn't that doing ministry was a terrible thing, but when it became my priority, it became a problem. Keep in my mind, I'm not speaking about my intimate time with God, I'm being specific to the works of ministry. When the works for the Lord became more important than your spouse and family relationships, it can cause much pain.

The major trap that Vincent and I had fallen into is the deception that marriage and ministry are separate. They're not. Marriage is ministry and ministry is marriage. Think about it. Both are compatible, not conflictual. At least, that should be the goal. Both take lots of time, energy, and effort to be successful. They are to be blended, not just balanced. I stated this because, when balancing, it appears there's a competition between two scenarios. Many leaders already feel that one area must suffer while the other thrives. We often feel that we have to choose between a good marriage and a good ministry instead of viewing them both as one. In my mind, the word "balance" involves a scale with which things are weighed, one versus the other, whereas the word "blend" involves togetherness, not separate, and not weighing one versus the other. So as a minister, I prefer the word "blend." My goal is to eliminate all competitiveness and merge both marriage and ministry together as one. While balancing makes them both equal, I believe God desires us to see ministry and marriage as one! Marriage and ministry were both created by God. They are both meant to be motivated by a love that is demonstrated in our service to those in our ministry as well as to our spouse. We are supposed to serve one another in love and give glory to God in all that we do.

The enemy was having us fighting each other blow by blow in the ring because we hadn't gained that understanding. Instead of viewing the two areas separately, we should purpose to view our marriages as our first ministries. So, if I am serving my spouse in love, which is ministering to him in love, then that should be reciprocated. When this happens, we are harmoniously combining the two components verses simply viewing them as balanced. Even in the natural, when two different elements are blended together, they become inseparable. A smoothie is a great natural example for this spiritual principle. Although the ingredients are balanced out, which means a certain amount of milk or fruit and/or vegetables are added to the blender, once those ingredients are ground together, they make one awesome smoothie. Once blended, you can't pick the fruit from the vegetables that have been placed in that milk, it becomes ONE!

Leaders in the church neglect their spouses and family more than people care to admit or address. Scenarios pop up in my mind of the countless first ladies that sit in service with a plastic smile on their faces, secretly resenting their husbands for putting the church first, or the disgruntled "PK's" (preachers' kids) who are once again disappointed because there was a needed counseling session at the church that outweighed their baseball game or recital. Those children are oftentimes rebellious because of the neglect. I also think of the angry husband whose wife is a minister and doesn't seem to remember to have fun in the bedroom or respect him as the head of the house. Maybe it's the scenario that plays out in my head of pastors who spend more time in the office with their assistant than they do with their spouse, which, in many cases, leads to an affair. All these scenarios are real stories that have developed and are developing even now, scenarios where God is not pleased. As a leader, we must realize that ministry is our call, but our marriage was our choice. Therefore, we must honor both as God does.

Drowning our marriages with excessive church talk and activities can be detrimental. The call of God is without repentance so even if our home is neglected, we can still see some level of results. The call doesn't change, but we also don't want it limited because we are neglecting our spouse and/or home. We must be Godly examples in the earth as Christian couples. Not balancing, not blending, and not compromising are all elements of hitting our spouse "below the belt," as they say in boxing. We must strategize and align ourselves with The Word of God so that when the enemy attacks our marriages, we won't throw in the towel. We don't want to end up in opposite corners against our spouse. The real opponent is the enemy, and it's time for us to knock him out!!

LET'S GET READY TO RUMBLE!!!!!!!!!!!!!

Lessons Learned

1. **Marriage versus ministry is an erred idea. They are one, just like you and your spouse.**

2. **Marriage and ministry both require time, energy, and effort to be successful.**

3. **Neglecting your home for ministry activities is not the will of God.**

2
MARRIAGE IS A NOUN, NOT A VERB

[19] *Now the LORD God had formed out of the ground all the wild animals and all the birds in the sky. He brought them to the man to see what he would name them; and whatever the man called each living creature, that was its name.* [20] *So the man gave names to all the livestock, the birds in the sky and all the wild animals.*

But for Adam no suitable helper was found. [21] *So the LORD God caused the man to fall into a deep sleep; and while he was sleeping, he took one of the man's ribs and then closed up the place with flesh.* [22] *Then the LORD God made a woman from the rib he had taken out of the man, and he brought her to the man.*

[23] *The man said, "This is now bone of my bones and flesh of my flesh; she shall be called 'woman,' for she was taken out of man."*

[24] *That is why a man leaves his father and mother and is united to his wife, and they become one flesh.*

²⁵ ***Adam and his wife were both naked, and they felt no shame. Genesis 2:19-25 (NIV)***

Marriage was the first union that God brought together in the Bible, the first institution that was founded in our human society—one male, *one female, coming together in a union to bond as one. Isn't it funny how, according to logic, one plus one equals two, but not according to God's standards? His intent, which is clearly stated in verse 24 of Genesis chapter 2, is that the two shall become one! I personally would laugh every time I ran my eyes across this verse, thinking, *God, you are hilarious if you think that Vincent and I could ever be one.* Vincent and I don't think alike. Our backgrounds are very different. He comes from a two-parent household, and I do not. He's athletic, and I'm not. He jokes around a lot, and I don't. He likes outdoor activities while I would rather stay indoors. As a matter of fact, as people say, "opposites attract," we were the poster kids for that campaign!

Marriage, from my point of view, was a solution to a problem that God detected when he looked at Adam after everything was created and saw that Adam had no other species that talked like him or looked even remotely the same. God felt that Adam needed a partner, someone who could relate to him and provide those missing pieces that Adam would need in the future—a companion to share love with and his life with—so God created Eve. God makes sure we are clear on her title in Adams' life because also in verse 24 of Genesis 2, God calls her "wife"—wife, which means Adam was a husband! God quickly identified who was what and what they represented, marriage. This union, of course, was not some casual dating scenario, nor was it a common-law situation; it was a union, a covenant in which two people were brought together —two separate creations of God to be joined together for a lifetime of becoming ONE.

We live in a society where people have become so skeptical about how they view marriage. Even the definition marriage has become cloudy. For some, the value of marriage has derailed and is not even on their goal list for life, and for others, it's just something to do. Because of the negativity that marriage is now associated with, it tends to scare many off, especially with high divorce rates that seem to be increasing every year. The saddest part of it all is that most of this information is being leaked by Christians, and our marriages have been put on public display for the world to see—the good, the bad, and the real UGLY!

In my heart, I know that God had great plans and intentions for our marriages when He created them, and I believe He still does. And even as you read about what almost ended as a disaster in my marriage, you will see that there is still a reason to trust that God's intent for marriage is for good.

One of the reasons that I personally believe marriages fail, or at least one of the reasons my second one was failing, is because people enter this union without understanding that marriage is a noun and not a verb. Personally, I always thought the opposite and had read several articles and even quotes that would lead me into feeling like it was all about what I do to make my marriage work, that if I could perform the right actions, they would override what my marriage had become—A DISASTER! My thoughts, like the thoughts of many others, was that marriage was something I needed to do right for it to be successful. I truly think very differently now as I glance back over Genesis 2:24. Do you remember the two-shall-become ONE-FLESH part? When we begin to understand that the words, "one flesh," in that Scripture are not referring to two human beings meshing together to physically become one person, we realize that the words, "one flesh," could simply have meant one team, one unit, or one alliance that God was building as they (male and female) continue to become. It would mean that the male gender and female gender, in their mind, heart, and spirit, would not see themselves as separate once they came together, but as consistently evolving together as one unit, becoming a totally different entity once their marriage started.

Let's look at the basic definition of these two words, and yes, I know you are far past grade school, but just humor me for a second.

According to Cambridge Dictionary, a **noun** is a word that refers to a person, place, thing, event, substance, or quality.

Also, Cambridge Dictionary defines a **verb** as a word or phrase that describes an action, condition, or experience.

In viewing these definitions with the thought that marriage is a sacred bond and covenant agreement, instituted by God, between a man and woman, then a marriage is who you are or become instead of something you do. A noun describes what something is while a verb describes what something does. For me, that means that marriage is not something I do, but who I am or become once I make those vows before God and man. Of course, marriage was set to be forever according to original biblical standards, which leaves me to believe my marriage will have lots of changes because my mate and I are two evolving individuals who strive to become one.

Looking at our marriages as who we are (a noun) changes the whole concept of how we react or respond (the verb) to our spouse. It also changes our concept of how we want to represent our one team, one unit, or one alliance, to the world. As I believed the Holy Spirit introduced this perspective to me, I had to begin to think differently. I had to begin self-inventory to figure out what I was presenting to those who were looking at my marriage. I begin to see that how I handled my marriage was how I handled myself! I began to see that the way I responded to this so-called "one team" reflected the brokenness that I saw within myself.

I realize that I am neither an English teacher nor an English major, but let's look at the basic definition of an adjective.

According to Cambridge Dictionary, an **adjective** is a word that describes a noun or pronoun.

A reason this is important as it pertains to marriage is because the words we use to describe our marriages will produce actions that demonstrate our marriages. If your marriage is a noun what is your adjective? "How would I describe my marriage?" Honesty is essential to taking your marriage to a higher level. Being honest, first with yourself, is key to developing what you desire to see even if it's not looking so good right now. My goal is to shift you into viewing marriage as who you are instead of what you do!

Considering that divorce rates, especially in the Christian community, are over 50 percent, I believe it would be safe to say that many viewed their marriage as an unhappy one. Words like discontent, horrible, irreconcilable, unhappy, etc. were being used to describe how they saw their marriages, which produced an action that pushed them into divorce. Divorce may not have been the only option, but these couples saw it as the one they would take.

How we view a situation will determine how we react. Our perspectives always produce a harvest in our lives because our actions follow what we say, and what we say follows our thought patterns. It is vitally important that we govern and use the authority that God has already given us to produce what we want to see manifested in our lives verses continuing to be negative due to what we physically see that's already there.

Seeing your marriage as a noun will also make you, as a partner in this union, accept accountability for how you are representing your team. Accountability is the acceptance that we have a part in what this marriage has become, and if we are not satisfied, we must do something to change it! Although God stated, "The two shall become One Flesh," that does NOT mean He will do all the work. Through His written word, God simply gives His expectations of the desired result of this union. It is up to us to determine how we will get there.

Getting there requires an honest and deep self-evaluation. Accountability in your marriage introduces an obligation to be the best partner you can be on this team. Even if that means changing or adjusting in an area to produce a better "US." This is not always the easiest process, but it is one that is required for change. Blaming your partner for all the issues that have gone wrong will not fix your problems. As a matter of fact, it will make things worse.

If you take pride in who you are as an individual, then you will operate the same way as a couple. When coaching other couples, one of the first things I listen for is the accountability on both ends. I want to hear which part they individually feel they are responsible for in the demise or issues pertaining to the marriage. I don't outright ask that question. I simply listen to how they express what's going on, and usually, they will let me know very quickly who they believe is at fault. I have very rarely encountered an individual in a marriage who outright, without any sarcasm, says, "It's all my fault," or "I am to blame for it all." Rather, I have found quite the opposite. It's human nature to blame the other person, right? But once accountability steps in, it causes you to be more self-aware and helps you work on the adjectives you use to describe yourself. This is because accountability filters through the issues in your marriage and helps you understand that you need change in order to survive your rough patch.

Accountability reminds us that we need to look at how we define our marriage (the noun), which will lead us to action (the verb) for desired results.

Lastly, as I view my marriage as a noun, I lend my attention back to the Scripture, Genesis 2:23a, Adams' words, "This is now bone of my bones and flesh of my flesh." This is true according to the Bible, but may I speculate that Adam felt this in his spirit and in his emotions as well, thus creating an inseparable bond? If this is so, according to my speculations, when we begin to view our marriage as one person and that both male and female as inseparable because of the covenant, wouldn't we be more cautious as to how we respond or react to and towards our partner? Wouldn't we be more kind, more merciful, more loving, and more forgiving because what we do to our partner, we are doing towards ourselves? Our actions would dictate how we feel about ourselves individually, which would reflect how we treat the person that we see as "bone of my bones." Only insane, immoral, or spiritually unhealthy people would harm themselves.

This is a perspective that I wish would have been a part of my premarital counseling because it would have spared my marriage a lot of issues. I would never knowingly slap myself or cut myself. Yet at times, I would knowingly use my word to hurt my spouse.
I would have thought more about how those unkind

words would hurt me as an individual instead of willingly inflicting them upon my spouse because I saw him as separate from myself. Remember, the point is to view your marriage as a noun so you can begin to produce the right actions. You are ONE with your spouse. In the eyes of God, you are a union, a team. What does your team reflect? Because hurting them is only hurting you.

Lessons Learned:

1. **My marriage is who I am (noun), not what I do (verb). By viewing it this way, I realize that the perspective I have of my marriage will help me produce my desired results through my actions.**

2. **Viewing my marriage as a noun versus a verb forces me to connect with my adjective and describe what I have created in this union. It also forces me to accept accountability, which means I may have to change or adjust to become a better "US."**

3. **Recognizing that my marriage is an inseparable bond helps me realize that I need to treat my spouse the way I treat myself. After all, he is me and I am him!**

3
GLASS HOUSE

"People who live in glass houses
should not throw stones"
Geoffrey Chaucer's Troilus

This proverb can be traced all the way back to 1385. Since then, there have been several other quotes that spiraled from this one that all had the same meaning. For instance, in 1651, George Herbert wrote, "Whose house is of glass, must not throw stones at another," and 26 years later, Benjamin Franklin wrote, "Don't throw stones at your neighbor if your own windows are glass." These men were introducing us to a phrase that opened society's eyes on vulnerability to the fact that all of us at some point will find ourselves in a state of need. The glass house, of course, was a figure of speech that was describing exposure, openness, and even a weakness.

Marriages expose our weaknesses whereas the dating process normally hides them. Couples usually don't see all of each other's weak areas clearly until they have gone down the aisle and the "I Do's" are now becoming "I Don'ts!" Spending time with someone occasionally is not the same as living under the same roof day in and day out. And trust me, even during your marriage, you both are discovering new things about each other; some you will like, others you won't.

Let me give you an example. Vincent and I dated 4 years before we were married. Every time I would visit his home, it was immaculate! For four years, I never saw a dirty tub or toilet seat—nothing, all spotless. After we were married, I discovered that Vincent doesn't like to clean the tub or shower right after he gets out, and that drove me crazy. There would be times when I was tired and was ready for "Calgon" to take me away, but I would walk into a bathroom with a dirty tub. I would have to clean it out or fuss because it hadn't been done. On the flip side of this, Vincent had never seen me argue much because we weren't around each other every day before we got married, but that had changed. We both were being unmasked and it wasn't funny.

We can turn the exposure into a positive in our marriages because they help us to learn how to be more patient with ourselves and our spouse. It also helps us to acknowledge that as individuals, we aren't perfect, but we can work through the differences. Lastly, the exposure helps us to learn more about each other so we as a couple can become one with each other. By turning this into a positive in your marriage, it means that you are now aware that there is a weakness and that you are working together to achieve a better result. For instance, if you found out your spouse has a weakness when it comes to overspending, instead of fighting over finances, you both can come together to create a budget for the household, one that you both agree on and that would allow compromise.

A major problem occurs with exposure when we use what we learn about each other as a weapon in our marriages. When we aren't so patient with our spouses' weakness and use each other's flaws to hurt one another. Let's look at the previous example about the one spouse overspending. Instead of coming together and creating the budget that includes compromise, the spouse that has the strength in finance is now badgering the spouse with the weakness. Instead of compromising and coming into agreement with each other, the door of contention and chaos has been opened. This leads to hostility and conflict.

I discovered, after reading the proverb mentioned earlier, that for some a glass house is considered a greenhouse. I am familiar with a greenhouse because my grandmother had one. It was, of course, all made of glass, which allowed everyone who passed by to see inside. She was growing various kinds of plants, and some were vegetables that we got to eat! I realize now that the plants were in a controlled and protected environment. This setting was intimate, exclusive, and private. Although you could clearly stand on the outside and view the results of what was happening internally. The environment and settings for our marriages are vitally important for the growth and strength of our relationships. My grandmother knew that too much heat in or out, too much sun, or not enough water would cause her plants to die. Her intention was to see growth and a harvest of beautiful flowers and vegetables to eat.

Our marriages are set up the same way, and no marriage is the same. As married couples, we must be sure to control what we allow into our marriages and set ourselves up for satisfactory results. The Bible makes it very clear that "The two shall become one," and one of the meanings I take from this Scripture is that there needs to be NO third-party interference in all your marital business. Adding outside opinions, especially if they are negative in your exclusive environment, may cause severe overheating, which results in plant death in a greenhouse (marriage). Privacy within the walls of your marriage is just as important as the amount of sunlight my grandmother allowed in that greenhouse. Without the right amount, her plants would have died, but we will talk more about this in a later chapter. As the owner, my grandmother made sure she did the necessary thing to keep her plants alive: she CONTROLLED AND PROTECTED! My grandmother didn't allow just anyone in her greenhouse, and we couldn't touch anything unless she said so! She even had a lock on it so that no one could get in without her permission. She took full responsibility for the well-being of each flower and plant that was in that greenhouse.

If we use the same parameters of a greenhouse and apply it to our marriages, we would see that our partner's exposure should be protected and covered by us in order that they may be nurtured properly. We should be praying and hoping for positive results, but if we're honest, many times it's quite the opposite and we lose ourselves in a war zone that could have been avoided.

Something made of glass can be easily broken, but with the rage and pain that was boiling in me towards my spouse, I didn't even care. As an individual, I always had a challenge with anger. My sister and other family that had experienced my wrath often called me "The She-hulk!" No, I didn't have the ability to turn green like the incredible hulk, but I would explode out of rage at the drop of a hat. It seemed as if I was angry with Vincent so much that I was becoming numbed inside day by day. I had stopped outwardly exploding, but I was now imploding. I was still boiling over with anger but was displaying it with a more nonchalant attitude towards him. Looking back and reflecting on my marriage, there were many occasions where I had no fear of the outside stones being thrown at my glass house because I had a brick in my hand ready to destroy it myself. Outside stones could consist of other's opinions or insults concerning our marriage. Those things didn't bother me at all. But my focus was directed to what was happening in me as our problems seemed to progress. This was not something that happened overnight, but gradually.

As our problems went unresolved, the more bitter I was becoming towards him. Bitterness is one of the results of unsettled anger, holding grudges against another person without forgiveness. I knew things were getting worse but didn't care to discuss. "Let the chips fall where they may" became my mantra. My attitude was a result of a pile up because we weren't creating solutions to our problems. Instead, we were just piling them on.

Within a few years of marriage, it seemed as if our greenhouse was looking more like an outhouse. The couple I had once known that was so madly in love seemed to have fallen off into a coma because our marriage was going downhill. Instead of being kind and considerate to each other, we were both vicious and rude. Instead of talking our issues out, we either had screaming matches or the silent treatment. Instead of being that hot, spicy couple in the bedroom, it was ice cold. And this behavior went on for months.

During that period of our marriage I realize that we were running into some serious challenges and possibly could have sought help for our issues, but we were both too prideful and stubborn. It seemed as if we were just letting it happen, and neither one of us cared enough to do anything about it. We were numb, stagnate, and frustrated, but did nothing. I was so angry that I wasn't protecting my marriage. Instead, I was assisting in its destruction.

To be aware of the tools that can help your marriage and not use them is sabotage. And to not know and not seek help is even worse. See, we both had been married before, so this was not our first try at this. We also had great marriage counselors in our pre-marital counseling, and if that wasn't enough, we surely had The Word of God to help us with our issues, but we were two Christians in a marriage that was exploding and imploding at the same time.

Unforgiveness, retaliation and awful communication skills had become apparent in our marriage, and the complexity of it was causing Vincent and I to grow further and further apart. I don't even recall how it all started, but the results were becoming more painful day by day. Pain is a perfect indicator that something has gone wrong, a trauma has or is happening, or a sure sign of discomfort is occurring. Suffering, agony, strain, struggle, hurt, torment, and torture are just a few associated with it. Pain can take place in many capacities of our life whether physical, social, emotional, financial, or psychological, and it can transpire in any area we allow it access. Pain can also be permanently damaging if not dealt with. Pain had welcomed herself in our glass house and began to take up space.

Keep in mind the ideal glass house is transparent, controlled, and protected. As I meditated on this thought, I realized that our marriages should be also. Transparency with your spouse is a vital aspect of a healthy relationship. Couples should really focus on their communication tactics with one another. There should be no pretense or deceit when talking with one another. We must learn to discuss issues with our spouses, even when they are uncomfortable.

Most people think that silence is a peacemaker, as if the problem or issue is going to just vanish when truthfully, that is so far off. Silence may be helpful depending upon the circumstance, but it can often lead to a road of pinned-up resentment when nothing is being spoken. Unspoken emotions can be dangerous and deceptive because your spouse has no clue how you feel. Because you hold it in versus being transparent about it, the glass house can no longer show whether what has been planted is dying.

Vincent was becoming more frustrated with my ministry schedule but wasn't communicating his feelings to me. My schedule included more travel for speaking engagements, and I was also writing my first book. My calendar was constantly filled with duties for our local church, being a mom, and working a full-time job, but I didn't slow down, although I knew he was agitated. While he was angry with me, I was also becoming more and more frustrated with his lack of communication about what was bothering him. I would continuously try to get him to talk to me because I could tell in his demeanor that he was upset all the time, but I had no luck. There were days when we would come home in the evening and not many words were being exchanged. As a matter of fact, I spent most of my time in our home office and he in another room. We were distant yet near, and it was becoming silently more hostile day by day. In front of others, we would put on our mask and play nice, but when the car hit the driveway of our home, the silence returned.

The lack of communication was breeding grounds for the spirit of unforgiveness to move into our "glass house" as well. Small offenses were not being addressed, and tensions were building. Our relationship went from lack of communication to bad communication.

When talking to each other about anything, the hostility would become present. There was criticism and stonewalling taking place in almost every conversation. Vincent's stonewalling tactics drove me crazy. He would delay and/or refuse to answer any questions that I may have asked him. For instance, if I asked how his day was, he would pretend that he didn't hear me talking to him. When asked again, he would give me a dose of his sarcasm. This behavior would trigger a critical spirit in me, and I was always ready for battle. I would start talking very loudly, and sometimes, name-calling would be involved. UMMM, yes—all of this took place in my Christian household. Our behaviors were very invasive to each other, and there were rarely any apologies.

Jesus addressed the disciples in Luke 17:3-4 concerning offense: *"Pay attention and always be on guard [looking out for one another]! If your brother sins and disregards God's precepts, solemnly warn him; and if he repents and changes, forgive him. ⁴ Even if he sins against you seven times a day, and returns to you seven times and says, 'I repent,' you must forgive him [that is, give up resentment and consider the offense recalled and annulled]."* (AMP)

Our glass house was no longer representative of a controlled environment. In a physical glass house, one of the owner's responsibilities is to make sure the room temperature, radiation, and humidity are measured for the plant life inside to grow. We were not growing spiritually in our marriage, and we were not growing closer together. Our attitudes were choking the life out of our relationship, and we were both watching it slowly die and not making any effort to fix it.

Our marriage was not only losing control and lacking transparency, but it was also not being protected. The Bible states this in *I Peter 4:8, "Above all things have intense and unfailing love for one another, for love covers a multitude of sins [forgives and disregards the offenses of others]."* (Amplified Bible, Classic Edition)

Instead of offering each other forgiveness, instead of covering each other in prayer, seeking counseling, or anything positive toward our union, we became retaliatory. It seemed as if we were in a war of who can hurt the other the most. Think about what I'm saying. We were a married couple, Christians, both preachers' kids, and still reflecting out of our flesh toward the person we were in a committed relationship with.

At this point, our pride wouldn't allow us to seek a divorce because we didn't want people to know we were having marital problems. Remember, we were pretending to be the perfect couple.

Our resentment toward each other was being openly displayed in front of our children. At this point, they were walking around the house tense and waiting for the next bomb to blow. Our youngest son was heavily affected because he was the only one home while the older kids were living in their own homes and/or off to college. Joshua's grades undeniably suffered as this once straight-A student was now bringing home C's. Joshua was also acting out at school his teachers because he was being rude and very disruptive during classes. Joshua also became more of a loner although he had normally been the excitable child who always enjoyed the company of others. It was also stressful coming home knowing that it would be another evening of not being spoken to, but my pride would say, "well, if he's not speaking to you, then don't you speak." I took on as many speaking engagements as I could, knowing it would bother him, and in turn, he would work lots of overtime to avoid seeing me.

We needed an intervention fast, but no one even knew we were having problems. How can you receive help when you won't even acknowledge to anyone that you need it? Our marriage was on life support, and there was no growth. Within a greenhouse there must be pruning for the plant life to grow and mature. Likewise, so should marriages. These rude habits that were being displayed by my husband and myself needed to be plucked out of us so that we could grow as a couple. Pruning is never an attractive process because it's the cutting off or trimming away of unwanted or unneeded branches. It's the dead stuff that needs to go so that the plant or flower can blossom to its fullest potential.

At this point of the relationship, we weren't mature enough to realize we needed pruning, so we sat right there in our glasshouse, each with a brick in our hands, waiting to see who would throw it first!

Lessons Learned:

1. **Marriages expose our personal weaknesses, but when processed correctly, they help us to be more patient with ourselves and our spouses.**

2. **Healthy marriages are like greenhouses. They both need transparency, a controlled environment, and to be protected.**

3. **Small offenses that are not addressed in your relationship become a potential threat that can destroy. Address them**

early so you can work on them before
they breed unforgiveness and retaliation.

4
THE RED FOLDER

"Many people only allow tragedy or disaster to be their teachers. That becomes a tragedy that can be avoided if we learn to see the signs early and be willing to do something about it!" ~Speak O

May 9, 2015 is a day I will never forget! I had just come home from a conference—a women's empowerment conference that I was a part of as I toured several states, ministering the Word of God to broken women. I often traveled with this group of ladies in hopes that we would minister a life-changing word that would cause deliverance and transformation in every listener's life. This was an awesome group of women that were very diverse in the gifts of the spirit, and we were all different and powerful in our presentation. The experience was more than amazing because it gave me an opportunity to operate in the calling of God on my life while simultaneously exposing me to traveling with a ministry.

I always left these conferences feeling refreshed and revived, renewed as if God had changed my perspective on life and given me another opportunity to come home and demonstrate my new revelations. I was so excited to come home despite all the chaos I had left behind, especially all the tension between Vincent and me. Right before my trip to St. Louis, we had had a major blowout, probably one of the biggest screaming matches we had ever had. I don't remember what it was about, but I know I didn't care as I traveled home because I was on my way to make up with my man.

I had such a huge smile on my face as I hopped in my car on my way home, just meditating on a word that I believe I had personally received from God in prayer. During the conference, I had ministered a word from the book of Esther, and my topic was, "There is Power in your Process." The gist of the message was to encourage the ladies that God has purpose in every trial, pain, and tribulation that challenges us and that God knows exactly which route we need to go through in life to see His blessings flowing. I surely wanted them to understand that many processes in life that we endure may not be comfortable and can often be painful, but each process was all planned out by God to empower and mature us for His will.

As I was driving home from the airport, I was filled with confidence that Vincent and I would be able to work out some of our marital issues. I was so overjoyed as I reflected on The Word of God that I had spoken to concerning there being power in their process. I, too, had that same authority for mine. The words that I had spoken into those women's lives God was now speaking back to me, and I was eager to get home to share this revelation with my husband. I was having flashbacks of happy moments we had shared: our wedding, the first time he asked me to marry him—on a hospital bed where he lay, full of morphine due to a car accident—vacations, and just times of laughter together.

All these memories were flooding my mind, and it seemed as if they were erasing all the harsh words we had recently been speaking to each other. I felt like the joy for my marriage was returning, and I was so encouraged that we would be able to mend our relationship.

As I pulled up onto the driveway to unload my bags from the vehicle, I realized I wasn't being greeted with welcoming arms. My son, Joshua, was gone with his father for the weekend, and the house was very quiet. I knew Vincent was there because his truck was parked, but there was a total silence that filled the home. This was strange for our house because there was always noise! My husband always had a TV or radio on nonstop, even when there were no children around.

This day was very different. I stepped into our bedroom, and there Vincent was, sitting in his recliner with a look on his face that I had never seen. It was bleak! His demeanor was very cold and unwelcoming! Honestly, I wanted to run and hide because I felt that, even without words, he wasn't looking forward to me coming home.

The tension, within seconds, became very thick, and as I've heard the expression, you could cut it with a knife—well, I would have needed a sword! I proceeded to say hello, and this is how the conversation went:

Vincent (sarcastically):"Glad you made it back home safely. Have a seat."

His tone was dry, no real concern and no question about how the conference went, just straight to his point as he was directing me to sit in my recliner.

Me: "It was great. I have some revelations that God showed me about myself and our marriage that I came home excited to share!"

I tried to put my smile back on my face and keep the conversation positive. His facial expression then shifted to this mean growl, and I realized that anger was bubbling up in him as he seemed to have ignored what I had just said and went straight for my jugular.

Vincent: "Orienthia, do you feel we need to be married? Because I don't!"

From nowhere, he pulled out this red folder and handed it over to me. Immediately, I was in shock by his words. I had the feeling of dizziness as if someone had literally hit me over my head. I was short of breath and couldn't believe the words that he had spoken.

Me: "Vincent, what are you talking about? Every couple has issues. We promised that we would always fight for our marriage. What is really going on here? Who is she?

This is not what I expected after the word God gave me!"

I was panicking and desperately trying to understand.

As I opened this red folder, sitting in the pocket on the left side was a divorce decree and on the right side an ink pen. Within seconds, my emotions went from panic to rage and then back to hurt and fear. I wasn't sure if I should cry or scream. I was devastated!

Vincent: "I don't want this marriage. And you can live here as long as you need to, but neither one of us are happy, and I want out! Maybe you can marry a preacher since you love ministry so much!"

Me: "So you don't want to get counseling or talk about it and try to work it out? Why are you being so hateful?"

There was no response as he walked away and slammed the door. I sat in that recliner for hours in silence, hoping that someone would wake me up from this nightmare. The truth is that it wasn't a nightmare or dream, it was my reality. This wasn't the fairy-tale life or marriage I wanted to have, but the reality of what I had built for five years. I was uncovered. I was unmasked. And I was confronted to now deal with my unraveling household that we had placed a Band-Aid on for five years! The pipes had now burst, and I was sitting there in the flood of my misery.

I remember being so grateful that none of the children were home because I couldn't stop crying. My mind was in so much conflict because, on one end, I was remembering what I believed God was saying to me concerning my marriage, and on the other end, I was remembering the words of destruction that we seemed to exchange in every argument. There was a battle in my mind, and the more I tried to think positive, resentment began to settle in.

Rage and resentment toward Vincent began to take residence in my heart. Their cousin, Pride, was at the helm of it. As the days began to pass by, I became more and more angry. We walked around that house as if the other didn't exist. Even in conversations with the children, we avoided our divorce news for at least a few weeks. They knew something was going on because less and less words were exchanged between Vincent and me. We also started doing less as a couple. Family dinners and family time was out of the question.

I secretly began to look for other living options because I hated coming to that house that I once called home every day. I knew that the home had belonged to Vincent prior to our marriage, and I wasn't going to fight against that in the divorce. My goal was to find a place for my two children and I. We are a blended family with a total of five children. His three were grown adults who lived on their own. I made up my mind that I would not sign these divorce papers until I was moved out and was comfortable in my new place. Vincent, however, consistently reminded me that there was no rush for us to move out, although he still desired a divorce. Most people would think that his offer for us to stay was kind, but my pride wouldn't allow me to remain in that house any longer than I needed to. As a matter of fact, I was frustrated and hurt daily because the home that was once filled with beautiful memories was now a pile of rubble.

I had no hope of reconciliation. The Bible says in Proverbs 13:12, *"Hope deferred makes the heart sick"* *(NIV)*. My heart was sick because it was filled with pessimism toward the man I once was in love with. It was sick because this was my second marriage, and I really wanted this one to work out forever. It was sick because I felt blindsided by Vincent's decision to serve me divorce papers, and my heart was sick from feeling like I was fighting with my husband with no resolve.

All I kept playing in my head was the amount of time I had wasted with him. By this point, we had been together nine years, four years dating and five years married, and I was now the one screaming that I wanted out! We had allowed deep-rooted wedges to divide us, and now we were so far apart that there was no turning back.

One of the wedges that pushed us to this place in our marriage was **avoidance**. Although we argued quite a bit, there was no real communication about any issues that would come up. Many times, we wouldn't sit down and thoroughly discuss our feelings concerning problems to each other. My husband loved to deflect in arguments, especially if I was trying to correct him or add a more unfamiliar perspective than his. For instance, Vincent was a fitness instructor, which means he would be around lots of women that had better shaped bodies than mine. I would notice that he wouldn't wear his ring in his class. That bothered me, and when confronted about it, his response would be, "It's no big deal." For me, it was a big deal, and every time I would mention it, it would cause a big blow-up between us in which he would counter about how I was around a lot of men when I did ministry. There would be no resolve at all, just another heated argument that would push me to a point of avoiding the issue all together.

Another wedge that separated us was **lack of respect** for each other. The signs were all there that we were being less respectful to each other as time went on in our marriage, but we did nothing to correct it. We had become great at cutting each other off while conversing. Sometimes, it would be so bad that not one full sentence would be completed by either one of us before it turned into a screaming match. If we weren't screaming, we were ignoring each other.

We often made our kids and friends uncomfortable with our criticism of each other and sarcasm. Over talking your spouse, ignoring your spouse, having the need to always be right, not considering the boundaries and feelings your spouse has communicated, and giving more attention and compliments to others, especially to those of the opposite sex, are all areas of disrespect towards your spouse and marriage. Vincent and I had all these issues and more going on, and we chose to ignore the hazard signs in our relationship as it was being destroyed.

There was no denying that we didn't see the issues, but how we expected to survive without even acknowledging them was simply ridiculous. If you're on a dark road and a sign says, "Bridge out ahead... Turn around," as a driver, you have a choice to make. You can obey the sign and prevent you and your passengers from unnecessary harm, or you can do it your way and ignore the sign, potentially leading the passengers to tragedy. The road signs are there to protect and prevent from harm, just like the signs we see in our marriages of things going wrong.

Vincent and I ignored the signs of lack of sex, the signs of neither of us making an effort to fix our problems, and the signs of our own selfishness and pride. As a result, I was moving out and divorce papers were on the table. This outcome had not been in my plans six years prior when we had said "I DO." I hadn't gotten married again to end up being a representation of another broken Christian family due to divorce. We were now a billboard for failed marriages, a disappointment to those who thought we had the perfect relationship, and a letdown to ourselves and our children.

That red folder represented the death of my vows, the assassination of my union, and the destruction of my hope of ever recovering to love again. My heart was shut down to Vincent and any idea of us bouncing back as a couple. I had survived my first divorce and was determined that after this one, I would never again open myself up so deeply to a man. I felt damaged and scarred in the same place, my heart. Tragedy had struck my home in the worst way, and now I felt so lost. I felt like a failure. God knew I wanted to change and be a good wife, but that dream was like shattered glass that was scattered in many directions on top of a red folder.

Lessons Learned:

1. Avoiding problems in your marriage doesn't fix them.

2. What God speaks to your spirit may not look like the reality of your situation. There is a process in between the problem to the promise.

3. Don't ignore the signs in your marriage that are exposing issues. Be willing to work through them together as a couple.

5
IT'S NOT FAIR

You didn't think, did you, that just by pointing your finger at others you would distract God from seeing all your misdoings and from coming down on you hard? Or did you think that because he's such a nice God, he'd let you off the hook? Better think this one through from the beginning. God is kind, but he's not soft. In kindness he takes us firmly by the hand and leads us into a radical life change. Romans 2:3-4 (MSG)

Months had gone by, and the kids and I were moving into our new residence. Vincent and I had managed to live together for two more months after the "RED FOLDER" was presented to me. My brother had recently begun leasing properties and had introduced me to one of his associates that had some nice homes for me to view. I had only looked at about six homes and was able to pick the perfect one so that we could move out. The process turned out to be so much easier than I had expected. It was literally unbelievable how fast the paperwork and approval went forth. I even found time to go pick out furniture and find movers within weeks.

I was relieved and finally ready to put my children in a less hostile environment.

It was a nice house, but it felt so strange and uncomfortable to me. It was affordable, it was very spacious, it had a nice yard, both front and back, it was a convenient location for Joshua to start his new school, and it was good for me concerning work and church. It was even nice to know my favorite mall was only five minutes away. Although my daughter, Lex, would be living on a college campus most of the time, I figured that when she would return during her summer vacation, she would even be able to find a job in the mall area in order to save up money. As a mother, I wanted to make sure my children were OK, although none of us were happy about this divorce.

I was totally disappointed beyond words as a parent because here I was, headed for another divorce, and my children were there witnessing this for the second time. They had already gone through my first divorce from their father, and now they had to deal with this one too. They were affected by this decision of course, but it seemed as if Lex and Josh were more concerned for me than for themselves. I have always been transparent with my kids, a quality that came with the privilege of them speaking freely yet respectfully on family matters. Neither of them could wrap their minds around what they thought was a perfect marriage now being dissolved. They would consistently remind me that they wanted me to be happy, and even though they loved Vincent, they realized I hadn't been happy during those last months. We were all ready to make this adjustment and simply get on with our new lives.

Although my marriage was falling apart, ministry, on the other hand, was going well and keeping me very busy. I had hired a brand manager who was also my graphic designer, and it seemed as if we were always working on another project. I can't help but chuckle to myself because, even in my despair with this marriage, God was allowing so many doors that represented victory in my life to open. I had written my first book, Really God?. I was a part of other book collaborations as well. I now had to keep a travel calendar for ministry because I was being invited more for speaking engagements. I started a prayer call that I hosted at 5am, three days per week. And I was rebranding the name and logo for my SpeakO Worldwide brand. I had also managed to complete my certification for my Coaching Services.

I was undeniably busy without complaints because it seemed to ease the pain of my broken heart. All these good things were happening around me, but I was separated from the man I loved. The person I so desired to be happy for me was no longer around. As long as I was busy with ministry stuff, I seemed to have been avoiding the emptiness I felt when things seemed to quiet down. I really missed my old home that had once been filled with love and beautiful décor that we created together. I missed Vincent's company. I missed the thought of being a wife and enjoying the comforts of having a husband. I missed seeing him and Josh playing basketball together or just talking loudly as they watched the games on television, constantly debating about who was the greatest basketball player of all time.

My emotions often overwhelmed me with grief as I would remember the good times Vincent and I once shared along with the talks that were so stress free. And the thought of the text messages that we exchanged throughout our work day would, for a split second, bring a smile to my face that would then lead me to a puddle of tears because they no longer existed. I cried almost every night in my bedroom or in my car coming from work in an effort to hide my true hurt from my children. I know that they knew I was hurting, but I just didn't want to add stress for them, and my pride wouldn't allow me to appear vulnerable.

I still had not signed the divorce papers because, as I stated previously, I wanted to make sure I was settled into a new place. After about a month in my new spot, I was ready to return Vincent's red folder to him with the signed documents. In my mind, since he refused counseling and made no effort to stop me from moving out, I figured there was no point in prolonging the inevitable. I added my signature and called for him to pick up the documents.

I was determined that this divorce was not going to break me, and when he came to pick up the papers, I wasn't nice to him at all. I quickly handed over the folder and told him I was looking forward to being single again. I didn't want him to know that I was already missing him. I did miss him, but my dislike for him weighed heavier on me. As he stood at the door, it seemed as if he wanted to say something, but whatever it was, I didn't want to hear it. I just wanted him off my porch. I didn't even allow him the opportunity to come in. My thought process was *take your papers and go!* I slammed the door, ran to my room, and cried like a baby.

My children knew that if my bedroom door was closed, that meant, "do not disturb unless the house is on fire or someone is dying." In other words, "leave me alone." There were many more of these moments to come because I was used to dealing with my problems by myself. And the place I had chosen for dealing with my problems was usually behind closed doors. I had great friends in my life and awesome family support, but I felt like no one could really understand my pain and frustration. Most of my ministry friends were happy with their husbands pastoring their churches or at least it seemed that way. My unmarried friends were all content in their singleness, happy, loving Jesus, and waiting on God to send their mates. Yet here I was, disconnected and significantly lost within myself, unsure of my identity. Should I refer to myself as a divorcee, a single mother, a separated woman, or what? I was a ball of confusion!

I was puzzled about many things at this point, but what I was certain of was the fact that I was angry at God—AGAIN! Yes, most people won't admit that, but that is the best way to express how I felt. I was angry at God for allowing my marriage to fail. I was angry at Him for not fixing the problems that I had brought before Him in petition for my husband. I was furious because of the embarrassment and scrutiny I would face being a single woman in ministry with children. I was livid because of all the slander and gossip from the church I attended about my separation; the news hadn't even been made public, yet they were gossiping already. This was just a compact list of venom that was pouring out of my heart.

The Bible says:
A good man brings good things out of the good stored up in his heart, and an evil man brings evil things out of the evil stored up in his heart. For the mouth speaks what the heart is full of. Luke 6:45 (NIV)

My heart was producing what it was full of, and there was nothing spiritual about it. My life had come full circle of what Vincent and I had harbored against one another in our hearts. This was what had brought us to this place of divorce. There was no more pretending. My marriage had crashed and was burning, and there was nothing I felt I could do to save it at this point. It was over! Emotions were overwhelming my mind, and I proceeded to have a major meltdown! I was cussing, crying, and banging on the floor with my fists, like a little child throwing a major tantrum. I recall looking up into a huge mirror that was attached to my closet doors and screaming these exact words, "Lord, why are you breaking me and not him?" I laid on the floor, waiting for God to answer, but I heard nothing—total silence as my tears continued to hit the floor. I must have been lying there for hours until I fell asleep in a puddle of shame.

Weeks went by, and I felt like damaged goods, like a broken vase that either fell off or had been pushed off of a night stand or the mantle of a fireplace. I felt like, every day, my assignment was to figure out how badly I was shattered and try to piece myself back together.

It seemed that none of my efforts were working and mostly because I was trying to do it on my own. It's funny how the enemy loves when we isolate ourselves from everyone. And due to my isolation, I was too prideful to ask for support.

Although I kept an active prayer life, I realized my prayers were not sincere. Most of my prayer time involved me still venting to God about everything my husband had done wrong to me. Looking back on it, you would think that a woman who was coaching other clients, presiding twice a week on her prayer call, and being in ministry for over 15 years would know better. On the other hand, I sympathized with myself because I was broken. My prayer time had become a 30-minute, or more, complaint session that included playing the victim to my circumstance. For some reason, I think I forgot that God was all-knowing and that He could not be manipulated. I think we all learn that truth, but we still act out as if we are not aware. God knew everything that had gone on, but I was only focused on my side of the story.

Playing victim to our circumstances is always easier than taking a deep look within ourselves. Initially, I was not ready to fully take responsibility for my part in the failure of this marriage, so blaming Vincent was easier. People who have a victim mentality are usually critical.

They are normally those who always see lack in their circumstances and usually don't trust others. I was wearing all these signs and more. I didn't realize that my failure to truly evaluate myself and make changes was one of the major reasons I was headed to divorce court. In my mind, everything was Vincent's fault, and I was determined to stick with that pattern of thought.

Due to this victim mentality that I refused to address, I ended up becoming very depressed. Oh, did I mention that I majored in psychology? I find it so ironic that I can major in a subject but not master it in my life. Some of the major signs I remember that led me to believe I was depressed include irritability, extreme fatigue, loss of appetite, feelings of sadness, and a lack of concentration. Every day, I would mask these signs with my ability to keep functioning and complete normal activities, all with a plastered smile on my face. At this point, few people knew what I was really dealing with behind closed doors.

Since I couldn't sleep at night, I found myself reading more. As a matter of fact, I had a habit of being in the bed with at least seven or eight books at a time. I think that was my way of dealing with the fact that after six years of marriage, I was, once again, alone in my bed. I had always been an avid reader, but at this point, I could just roll right over, pick any book, and start flipping the pages. My Bible was in this collection because, for some reason, it would always put me to sleep. I dare not say because it is boring, so I will say it gave me a peace that would allow me at least a few hours of sleep per night.

One night, during my sleepless moments, I was reading the Bible and then stopped right in my tracks. I felt as if the words from the pages were so magnified that I could not miss them. Honestly, I was horrified at the words because I was so guilty and felt so ashamed for my months of temper tantrums. I was CONVICTED, and my spirit was arrested! This was what I call a "Holy Ghost stick up." These are moments in which I feel as if God is saying, "I got you. Now deal with it!" This was the case as I read the following:

You didn't think, did you, that just by pointing your finger at others you would distract God from seeing all your misdoings and from coming down on you hard? Or did you think that because he's such a nice God, he'd let you off the hook? Better think this one through from the beginning. God is kind, but he's not soft. In kindness he takes us firmly by the hand and leads us into a radical life change. Romans 2:3-4 (MSG)

These Scriptures hit me like a ton of bricks! Immediately, my mind flashed back to moments when my character was not in alignment with The Word of God. I was seeing visuals of me pointing my finger in Vincent's face, me screaming to the top of my lungs at him, me throwing items across a room, me hanging the phone up in his face before he could get a sentence out. I was getting a heavenly download of my "ratchet" behavior over the course of six years, and it was nothing pretty. I was flooded with regret of how I had treated him. In this moment, I couldn't focus on all the wrong he had done. All I could see was myself. I had to deal with myself. I was being dealt with by the Spirit of God about MYSELF! For the first time in months, I was focused only on my own wrong. It's not that Vincent's wrong wasn't important, but I felt that in that moment, God was waiting on me to mature and be willing to see myself.

I often read The Message translation of the Bible because of the visual effects it has on my mind. When I read this Scripture, I saw a finger pointing at me. I felt in my heart that God was speaking to my spirit, that it was time to deal with myself, and I didn't need to keep justifying my wrong doings by bringing up Vincent's. In marriage, we can't grow spiritually if we are always using excuses for our actions, blaming them on our spouse. We must take responsibility for our actions and allow the Word of God to saturate our minds in order to cause positive change in our negative situations. At this point, my marriage appeared to be over, but I was still responsible for changing my ways because they were not reflective of a Godly woman.

It was time to do self-evaluation. It was time to deal with the reflection in my mirror, and that was going to take some tireless effort on my part. Although I was now focusing on myself, my mind kept referring to months earlier, back when I was pinned down to the floor and asking God why he was breaking me and not him (Vincent). God quickly shifted my thoughts to a small adjustment of my question. It was now, "Lord, why are you breaking me?" My question no longer included the mere thought of God's business and how He would handle Mr. Speakman.

I have heard people say we shouldn't question God. Well, I am one who totally disagrees. God is my creator, my Father, my provider. Why not ask Him, since He is all-knowing? I believe God wants us to ask Him questions so that He can direct us to His answers. As I began my self-evaluations, I found myself writing down my feelings, not in complete sentences, but just describing my feelings in words. By the way, I am a person who believes in journaling, but this exercise was separate from that. As I took pen to paper, I numbered my paper, and my list looked like this:

1. Broken
2. Disappointed
3. Disconnected
4. Worthless
5. Betrayed
6. Scarred
7. Humpty Dumpty

As I looked at my words and the tears began to flow, I chuckled and began reciting the nursery rhyme for Humpty Dumpty. You know it:

> Humpty Dumpty sat on a wall,
> Humpty Dumpty had a great fall;
> All the king's horses and all the king's men
> Couldn't put Humpty together again.

The words of Mother Goose were articulating exactly how I felt. The last sentence seemed to sum up my life. Who was going to put me back together? How would I be worth any value while being broken like this? How long would I feel like this? As all of these questions went unanswered in that moment, my search for the Scriptures on brokenness became a top priority on my list. I chose that word since it was first on my self-evaluation exercise, and I began to open my heart day by day in search of my healing. I knew it would be a long road, but I had a mind to change and a heart to want to please God even if my marriage didn't work.

In studying brokenness, I was finding relief because I realized that God was near to the broken hearted. Psalm 147:3, Isaiah 66:1-2, and Isaiah 61:1 became daily reads as a reminder of God's love for those who are broken and how His intent is to heal, set us free, and deliver us from that state of being. I know that the Word of God is always a source of encouragement because, remember, I'm a preacher, teacher, and transformation coach. The Word of God is always a reference source that I direct others to in their time of need.

During my personal research, I was enlightened by a principle that I had never seen before, and it truly changed my whole perspective on brokenness. It's a philosophy called kintsugi. "In his devotional, Abiding in Him, author Jimmy Larche explains that..."Kintsugi is basically the art of seeing value in broken things." The story of kintsugi is said to have begun in the 15th century, when Japanese military commander, Ashikaga Yoshimasa, broke one of his beloved Chinese tea bowls. Disappointed with the shoddy repair job, he urged Japanese craftsmen to come up with a more pleasing method of repair. The craftsmen decided to use gold in the fractured pieces to seal it back together. When completed, the bowl had now tripled in value due to its repair!

This philosophy treats breakage and repair as part of the history of an object, something of a redemptive beauty as opposed to something to disguise, cover up, or replace altogether. It's a worldview that sees beauty in the flawed, the damaged, or the imperfect. The idea behind the technique is to recognize the entire history of the object, with all of its cracks and flaws, and to visibly incorporate the repaired fissures into the new piece. It beautifies the breakage and treats it as an important part of the object's history, thus valuing the fractures instead of disguising them or glossing over them. The process typically results in something far more beautiful and elegant than the original. To throw the broken pot away is to destroy its unique story. To repair it the kintsugi way is to continue its tale of adventure, triumph, and redemptive beauty. This principle ministered to me because it gave me hope that even in going through this divorce and feeling flawed, broken, and irreparable, this was not my end destination. This principle encouraged me through the reminder that though I was broken now, God was not throwing me away; He was making me more valuable through my flaws. I realized that I no longer felt the need to hide what I was going through with my family and close friends. Instead, I needed to expose my issues in order to truly heal.

I realized that there is truly a beauty that is discovered when we begin to realize that God is using everything in our lives, including our brokenness, pain, failures, weaknesses, fractured relationships, shattered dreams, betrayals, cracked personalities, and scars, to bring about a beautiful, redemptive story. He is making all things work together for good for those who are called according to His purpose. I knew in that moment that my life was not over. God was doing a new thing, and I couldn't wait to see what that looked like. I didn't have to throw away any part of it. My testimony was being developed the moment I received this revelation.

Lessons Learned:

1. **Our actions and lives are a product of what we have stored in our heart. Look around you. Your manifestation came out of your heart.**

2. **True healing comes with real acknowledgement of the issues. You can't fix your marital problems by blaming your spouse. The work begins when you are honest with yourself concerning your role in the problems.**

3. **Our brokenness adds value to our lives. God wants to use every flaw, disappointment, betrayal, failure, and even fractured relationship as a testimony after you have been healed. Stop hiding your scars and allow them to help others receive their breakthrough.**

6
WHEN NAOMI STEPS IN

One day, Naomi said to Ruth:

It's time I found you a husband, who will give you a home and take care of you.

² You have been picking up grain alongside the women who work for Boaz, and you know he is a relative of ours. Tonight he will be threshing the grain. ³ Now take a bath and put on some perfume, then dress in your best clothes. Go where he is working, but don't let him see you until he has finished eating and drinking. ⁴ Watch where he goes to spend the night, then when he is asleep, lift the cover and lie down at his feet. He will tell you what to do.

⁵ Ruth answered, "I'll do whatever you say." ⁶ She went out to the place where Boaz was working and did what Naomi had told her. Ruth 3:1-6 (CEV)

Ruth and Naomi—they're a dynamic duo in the Bible that is usually mentioned because of Ruth's marriage to Boaz. It's a story in which all seems lost, but as you continue to read, you learn that the contrary is true. It's a powerful and orchestrated work of God without any mention of His name. Seriously, even without the mention of His name, you see God's handiwork as you turn each page of the story. I am always amazed at how many look at this powerful text as though the lesson they can pull from it is solely wrapped around a widowed woman finding love again.

Truth be told, up until the shattering of my marriage and my meeting of my spiritual mother, I too, was one of those people who only saw the text from such a point of view. I had overlooked Naomi's importance because I was distracted by the romance. God would often minister to my soul as my flesh was raging with questions. He began to direct me to reread the book of Ruth. My first response was, "Lord, the book of Ruth is a love story about how a single woman can catch a good man. What does that have to do with my broken marriage? How does this apply to me when I'm going through a divorce and not even sure if I ever want to be married ever again? How can this book of the Bible help my heart to heal and move on?"

My questions, of course, were not immediately answered because, as we know, usually, without many details, God has a way of making us go through hard processes to open our spiritual understanding. He has a plan that He is weaving into our pages of life as another beautifully orchestrated work! Let me simply encourage you with the reminder that even during our heartache, God's plan is always for us to grow and learn through our experience so that we may help others!

The separation from my husband along with the emotional trauma from being at the door of my second divorce opened my spiritual eyes to see Naomi's role in Ruth's life as one of much importance. Of course, Naomi had value in the story—after all, she's mentioned throughout it—but for me, Naomi's mention had not been vital until God began unveiling new revelations for me. It's hilarious how I'm realizing that Scripture is truly alive! Oftentimes, right when that word is desperately needed, it appears to shake you in your spirit as if it's screaming, "WAKE UP AND PAY ATTENTION!"

Late one night, I decided to stop delaying and start reading. I knew I had heard God speak those instructions to my spirit, but I just didn't want to read a love story while my heart was broken. As I began to read, I noticed this time was very different. I began to view Ruth's story from a mother-daughter perspective. I began to see the seriousness of their relationship and how unique it was to Ruth's fate! In my mind, as I read Naomi's words and instructions to Ruth, I realized that it was because of those instructions that Ruth got her Boaz!

I remember thinking Ruth was a single woman whose marriage ended due to her husband's death. Mine was a marriage headed toward divorce. Ruth had an awesome relationship with her mother-in-law, and the relationship I had with mine was strained because of the soon-to-be divorce. I had a mother that I could go to, but I was so hurt and lost that I didn't want to talk about my issues only to stress her out more! These thoughts were making me more frustrated than ever, but I kept reading and studying the book of Ruth.

I find it funny, as I'm reflecting on these moments, how it seems as if my spiritual mother just popped into my life out of nowhere! I am so grateful for social media because this is how we met. To make a long story short, she instructed me to call her in a private message. I normally don't respond to this type of messaging, but her wording struck a chord in my spirit, and I felt compelled to just hear her out. I was so sarcastic at the time that I had decided I would just hang up on her if I didn't like what she was saying. Mind you, this was after I had looked through all her photos, went to her website, and read up on her, her husband, and their ministry. It was strange indeed, but I knew God had to be up to something!

The call started out very interestingly as I heard this very cheerful woman on the other end of the line. Her tone and laughter seemed as if she had known me forever. I was cautious in my responses back to her, and then she says, "God has been calling your name out in my spirit for weeks. He has shown me things that are going on in your marriage that you haven't shared publicly, and only few family members are aware!" Tears flowed down my face as I felt every wall that I had set up against her come crumbling down. I knew it was God. She simply began to pray for me. She asked if she could check in on me again. Although I could hardly respond, I barely managed to get a "yes" out of my mouth before I hung up the phone.

All kinds of thoughts went through my mind, but I knew it was God. I couldn't get her words out of my head. I felt a sense of longing to hear her voice. It was comforting to me, although at this point, I had only heard it once. It was different than talking to one of my spiritual sisters. It was more authoritative yet sweet with a plethora of wisdom, especially in the areas where I needed it most. Momma Carol was a woman of her word because, the next week, she called to check on me and pray. The third call went a little differently because I felt led to ask her to mentor me and to be my spiritual mother. She began to cry this time as she revealed to me that God had already spoken to her heart about it. It was settled. I now officially had opened my heart to having a spiritual mother again. I had been damaged in this area before and had locked out even the idea of one, but this lady was special, and I knew I needed her for this next phase of my life.

As my relationship with Momma Carol began to blossom, my studying of the book of Ruth intensified. Instead of seeing the differences in my life and Ruth's story, I now was beginning to see similarities. Naomi taught Ruth many principles that I'm sure not only helped her obtain Boaz's attention but helped her keep it after their vows. These principles had nothing to do with the outward appearance; rather, they had to do with Ruth's character and ethics that made her glow even brighter.

The first principle that Momma Carol and I established in our relationship was loyalty and commitment to each other. I began to realize that, as women, many of us are ready to establish this in a marriage or with a dating partner but have never taken the time to value it in a female-to-female relationship. Ruth's priority was not looking for Boaz after she lost her first husband. It was making a commitment to be loyal to Naomi, a woman who had influenced her life greatly. Ruth chose to stay, even when Naomi had nothing visible to offer her. She could have walked away like Orpah, but she clung to Naomi even more. Let's look at the text:

14 They cried again. Orpah kissed her mother-in-law goodbye, but Ruth held on to her. 15 Naomi then said to Ruth, "Look, your sister-in-law is going back to her people and to her gods! Why don't you go with her?"

16 Ruth answered, "Please don't tell me to leave you and return home! I will go where you go, I will live where you live; your people will be my people, your God will be my God. 17 I will die where you die and be buried beside you. May the LORD punish me if we are ever separated, even by death!" Ruth 1:14-17 (CEV)

Ruth's commitment and loyalty to Naomi was vowed even unto death. I began to see that while this principle was going in my relationship with Momma Carol, it had been lacking in my marriage. The mirror was now placed in front of my face, and I wasn't liking the reflection. At some point during my marriage, I forgot where my loyalty should have been. I was more committed to my children, my ministry, and my projects, so my husband had fallen further down the line.

As a newly separated woman, Momma Carol kept me focused on being loyal and committed to my marriage even though divorce papers had been signed. She continuously reminded me that I was a married woman and that her goal was to believe God to mend it, even when I had given up hope. I was learning how to be committed to my spiritual mother. As a matter of fact, I was committed to both of my spiritual parents because Papa Nick also gave me counsel during this time. I believe that my commitment to them somehow made me desire that type of commitment for my marriage. I had begun to realize that my loyalty and commitment to Vincent hadn't been communicated through my words or actions in our union, but I was able to show loyalty and commitment to my spiritual parents with no problem. As I reflected on this fact, I realized that this was an issue because I should honor my husband the same way, but I hadn't.

Oftentimes, we forget the Scripture in Song of Solomon 2:15, *"Catch the foxes for us, the little foxes that spoil the vineyards, for our vineyards are in blossom."* I often say it's the small foxes that spoil the vine, which I believe means that it's the little issues we fail to see that normally bring about a bigger issue when not addressed. For example, when Momma Carol would call me on the telephone, I was dropping everything else to make sure I gave her the needed attention during that call. My attitude and voice tones were almost always pleasant. And even in moments when she would be correcting me or giving me information that I didn't like so much, I was still welcoming to her. On the other hand, the Holy Spirit began to show me the opposite in my actions when I would receive a call from my husband. I was always rushed and often rude to him when he called. And heaven forbid he try to correct me or tell me about things I didn't want to hear, or else, I would EXPLODE! And to be very candid, there would be moments I didn't even answer the call. Sounds simple, right? But small issues like this display a lack of commitment to our spouse if we are putting others first and treating them better. It can make a spouse resentful, and I had never seen that before. I began to recognize that I wanted to give my husband the same loyalty and commitment that I displayed in my relationship with others, the relationship I deemed important to me.

The second principle that began to bless me through this relationship was accountability. As a mentor/mentee to each other, Momma Carol and I put some expectations of each other in place as well as some boundaries that we would not cross with each other. I was glad we had had this discussion early in our relationship because I had been previously wounded in this area. I was shaky going in, but I was loving how God had placed us together, and I wanted to do my part by being a good mentee. We were accountable to each other spiritually, and I wanted it to be demonstrated appropriately through both of our lives.

Accountability, to me, simply meant to accept or be obligated to something or someone. I was now attached to a woman who I saw as a spiritual covering for my life; that included my marriage and my ministry. We put simple parameters in place such as a weekly call that would be devoted to conversation and prayer. She made sure she received an update on what was taking place with Vincent and me. Within weeks, she was investing in my life, not only through phone calls and prayer, but she was sending me literature that she thought I needed to read and study. I, on the other hand, appreciated feeling the love of a spiritual mom and was so thankful for her time and how our talks were helping me that I started sowing a financial seed in her and Papa Nick's church. As months went on, we knew each other's family and began preparing to meet in person. Oh, I never mentioned that God sent me this jewel all the way from the West Coast even though I reside on the East!

Ruth and Naomi displayed the accountability to each other in the Scripture.

⁸ Boaz went over to Ruth and said, "I think it would be best for you not to pick up grain in anyone else's field. Stay here with the women ⁹ and follow along behind them, as they gather up what the men have cut. I have warned the men not to bother you, and whenever you are thirsty, you can drink from the water jars they have filled." ¹⁰ Ruth bowed down to the ground and said, "You know I come from another country. Why are you so good to me?" ¹¹ Boaz answered, "I've heard how you've helped your mother-in-law ever since your husband died. You even left your own father and mother to come and live in a foreign land among people you don't know. ¹² I pray that the LORD God of Israel will reward you for what you have done. And now that you have come to him for protection, I pray that he will bless you." Ruth 2:8-12 (CEV)

It was Ruth's accountability to Naomi that made Ruth go find work in the field to ensure they didn't starve. She wanted to take care of Naomi the best way she could. Naomi may not have been able to provide for Ruth in the same way, but her wisdom and instructions to Ruth still served as provision from her end. They were two women who had lost everything except for the love to help each other.

Ruth's accountability to Naomi positioned her to become the center of attention for Boaz. He had heard of how Ruth was caring for Naomi even after their husbands had died, and he was impressed. He was also captivated by the fact that Ruth had walked away from her own people to be with Naomi. Accountability brings on an obligation, an oath towards someone or something outside of yourself. Ruth confirmed this in her actions, and this character trait got her noticed. Boaz was doing his research on Ruth as she was being accountable to her mother-in-law, and it made him pray a special blessing over her life.

My concluding principle to share in this chapter is submission and obedience. OUCH! I know those hurt! My flesh never liked those words, and combining them in my head was impossible. I must continuously view these words as a heart check for myself. I have grown to understand that individuals' attitudes towards what's being asked of them is the separation between those two words. Many believe that submission and obedience are the same, but let me share a distinct perspective. Submission is coming under the authority of another, to willingly surrender your power to that individual, in some cases, even when you don't agree. Obedience is dutiful compliance to the command of another. Submission involves willingness while obedience involves obligation. Both are needed. I will even go further to give this example. Imagine having two children, one boy and one girl. You give both the command to clean their rooms immediately. The girl goes right in and begins cleaning. As a matter of fact, she's humming her favorite song while doing it. The boy, on the other hand, is murmuring and tossing items around as if he is displeased with the given instructions. Both are cleaning, which represents obedience, but the separation line is in the attitude that represents submission. The girl is humming, and the boy is murmuring. The girl's submitted because she has willingly surrendered to authority, which is displayed in her peaceful attitude with the command. On the other hand, the boy is reflecting his discontentment by his actions.

In your mind, you're probably needing an example for your marriage. Let me tell on myself—and don't you laugh at my pettiness. Often, I would go grocery shopping for the household, and due to my busy schedule, I would do it on specific days—Tuesday and some Saturdays if needed. Vincent, I believe on purpose, would seem to call me on a different day or as soon as I would walk out of the store requesting me to pick up an item. On one specific occasion, I remember hanging up on him abruptly and then storming back into the store with attitude and getting the deodorant he asked for. As I arrived home and threw the deodorant on his dresser before he arrived, I heard the Spirit of the Lord say, "You obeyed, but you are not submitted. He asked you to do a simple task that may have seemed out of your way, but it was to expose your heart. How many times has he gone out of the way for you with no complaints?" My soul became grieved, and I began to cry as I saw my selfishness. I did the act (obeyed), but my attitude was foul (not submitted). These types of scenarios opened my eyes to the difference in obedience and submission and how my actions would display the difference. I am still striving for perfection, but I'm very proud of the fact that I am so much better. Remember what the Bible says:

[19] "'If you are willing and obedient, You shall eat the best of the land; [20] But if you refuse and rebel, You shall be devoured by the sword.' For the mouth of the LORD has spoken." Isaiah 1:19-20(AMP)

Ruth displayed both submission and obedience in her connection with Naomi. In studying the Scripture, I have yet to see a moment in which Ruth complained or felt displeasure with the instructions that she was given. Ruth constantly bowed to the words of her mentor, and this has been my heart toward Momma Carol. Ruth trusted Naomi, and because of that bond, she was able to submit and obey. Look at this demonstration of Ruth's submission and obedience to Naomi, keying in on verses 5 and 6:

[5] Ruth answered, "I'll do whatever you say." [6] She went out to the place where Boaz was working and did what Naomi had told her. Ruth 3:5-6

My relationship with Momma Carol has created this same environment in our connection, one of trust, where I have felt safe submitting and obeying her wisdom. Considering that Momma Coral had spent more than 25 years as a wife, I felt comfortable in listening and following through on principles she would openly share with me. Her words were beginning to change my thinking toward my husband in this very area. My marriage began to heal, and although we were living separately, I was able to activate these disciplines.

I remember a certain conversation that Momma Carol and I were having concerning my marriage. She was telling me to stop being so snappy with Vincent, to be kind. My attitude began to boil, but I remained silent as she was speaking. I kept thinking, "Has she forgotten what this man has done to me?" But I listened. The more she talked, the more my spirit went from murmuring to calm. Suddenly, I heard a lawn mower in my backyard. It was Vincent outside of the home I was renting. He was cutting my grass! I was in shock! Why is this man outside of my home, cutting grass? As I told Momma Carol, she simply said, "Daughter, be kind. He still loves you, and you still love him. Take him some water and say thank you."

I sat there for a moment, and I surprised even myself by getting up and obeying Momma Carol's instructions. Vincent was even amazed to see me walk out on the back patio towards him with water and a towel. Not many words were exchanged at that moment. I simply said, "Thank you" and went back into the house. He stood there for a minute because I didn't hear the lawn mower cut back on until I was out of sight. He felt comfortable enough to call me that night. He wanted to know who had been talking to me because my response to him was very different than the usual I had been giving him since the separation. My response was, "My Naomi has stepped in my life."

In conclusion, to have a spiritual mother/mentor has been an absolute blessing to my life. To feel that I have a woman who is full of wisdom, especially in this area where my life was hurting, has made a tremendous difference. I've always surrounded myself with women I called my sisters in Christ, but I had to open my heart for someone to sit in a seat of authority and who could give me directions and guidance through my process. I had horizontal relationships: sisters, side by side. However, I needed a vertical relationship: mentor/mentee, one I could reach up to. I am not here to convince but to testify about how God blessed me with this type of bond, one that reflected the story of Ruth and Naomi's connection. Naomi was not Ruth's sister, but she was a mother figure to her. Such a relationship is interchangeable and not just beneficial to one side. When Naomi (Momma Carol) stepped into my life, it impacted my relationship with my marriage. I am the Ruth in this story, and I did get my Boaz back. I believe one of the reasons was because I opened myself up to receive from the gift that God had brought into my life. God gets all the glory, but I honor her. She is still being that example I need, and I am truly grateful.

Before closing this chapter out, I want to make it very clear that a relationship with spiritual parents/mentors should not be one of dictatorship. Boundaries must be set and respected by both parties. They present information and suggestions, but it is always your choice as to whether you will receive and implement. Many times, the information wasn't presented in just conversation by my spiritual parents, but they were living it out in front of me. Momma Carol has a saying: "Daughter, some things are caught while others are taught!" She wanted me to understand that it may not be by her words that I understand, but by her actions. This has become very important to me because it helped me realize that she wasn't trying to boss me around with her words and manipulate me through Scripture reference. Instead, she opened her life for me to watch her actions. I saw how kind she was to her husband and his kindness back toward her, how soft spoken she is when he's requesting something of her, how she responded to adversity that came in her life, and even how she responded to the attacks of others. I watched her, and because my spirit was able to see The Word of God mirrored in her life, the trust began to build in our relationship.

No two marriages are alike, so even when she and I would communicate, I would still go to God in prayer for myself and allow my spirit to lead me. Be sure to ask God who is suitable for you and your spouse as a spiritual covering/mentor. Test their words and actions by the Word of God. Keep in mind, your marriage is yours, and the best third party is GOD, but good counsel is a blessing and will enhance your relationship. When this war broke out in my marriage, it was a great feeling knowing that I had some extra help fighting in this battle.

Lessons Learned:

1. God will often use trial, tragedy, and trauma to open our spiritual awareness within ourselves.

2. Be willing to receive or accept the spiritual authority that God is bringing in your life to help heal your marriage or another broken area of your life.

3. Loyalty and accountability, along with submission and obedience, are needed in a successful mentor/mentee relationship as well as in your marriage.

7
OUTLAWS, IN-LAWS

"True oneness in marriage cannot be experienced if you allow in-laws to penetrate the circle. If necessary, let them become out-laws. It is crucial that you establish boundaries."
— **Deborrah K. Ogans,** *How Do I Love Thee: Food for Thought Before You Say "I Do"*

This separation was very hard for me of course, but one of the major reasons was because I was consistently having to see Vincent more than I wanted to. We both attended the same church, and it was also a church that his father had founded. Yes, a family church where lots of members have the last name, Speakman. Now, many have asked me, "Well why didn't you just leave and find another church?" For me, that wasn't so easy because I have always been very dedicated to the call of God on my life. I was the pastor of Christian Education and the president of the Next Level Women's' Ministry. In other words, I was heavily tied to the operations and programming in this ministry. I felt as though I was already a part of the disappointment of our marriage falling apart, but I didn't want to add more damage as I thought that my leaving the church would affect other members of the church and maybe cause them to leave as well. I wasn't planning to add a church split to my plate at this time, so I prayed about it and decided to stay and remain active in my role.

The separation allowed me to have the space and room to reflect on many of the areas that went wrong in our relationship. In my heart, regardless of what was happening in marriage number two, I still believed with all my heart that I was fit to be a good wife. Maybe I had simply married the wrong people. I was still desiring marriage—just not this one!

Marriage, as I have stated previously, is already challenging work with just the husband and wife trying to deal with the everyday pressures of life and still be at peace with each other. But I discovered that keeping people out of our marriage, or in other words, keeping proper boundaries, was vital. I realized that having family, friends, and social media in my marital business had caused more headaches and heartaches than I had bargained for! While on the other hand, it helped to be able to have a few people who were non-judgmental and helpful.

Marriage is primarily between the two people who spoke their vows to one another, yet it is also inclusive of the significant other's family, friends, and children who were in his or her life before the spouse came along. In other words, it is my belief that when you marry your significant other, you also accrue additional people who you now are involved with, whether you want them or not. They come with the territory, and many of us don't consider that before the "I Do's." The problem for most of us who are married is not so much of the fact that we have accrued the additional family members and friends, but we often don't know what to share with them or what not to share as it pertains to our marriages.

I am a firm believer in the idea that not all ears are the right ears for your marital issues. Vincent and I had serious problems in this department, and it really surfaced or was uncovered during the separation. We had not done a good job with keeping people out of our business, and it was our fault! We had not guarded our relationship, and we had invited many of the wrong family members and friends into our marital chaos. Looking back, we realize that just because they were family didn't mean they needed ALL the details of what was happening in our home.

As I stated briefly in an earlier chapter, guarding your marriage is your responsibility. What the two of you allow in your union is solely your doing. Picture a closed fence around a property with a sign that says, in bold letters, "No Intruders." This means that the owner of that property has the authority and right to keep others out unless they're invited in. The fence is providing boundaries—a word that many people don't like to say and one they find is even more difficult to implement in their relationships.

Boundaries point us in the direction of ownership. They determine who's responsible for what. In a union, although we are striving to become one, we must accept responsibility for creating a marriage that has the proper fencing. This means that we as individuals must be able to assess ourselves and our behaviors so that we are empowered to change if need be. When we learn how to assess properly, we become more actively involved in resolutions to our marital issues rather than becoming a bigger problem. Before we talk about keeping others out of our marriage, we must figure out what should be kept inside.

Boundaries represent the limits or rules for something, a separation line that states what goes or doesn't go in an area pertaining to our marriage. Many of us had no clue how to set these boundaries because we come into our union head over heels in love, not even thinking about the problems that may arise because we have not openly discussed the "No Goes." The privacy of your problems that may arise have to have boundaries set in place or they will prove to be a recipe for disaster.

Involving third parties in my relationship matters exploded in my face, and it seemed to be a bigger challenge than just the issues we were already dealing with. Nasty, vicious rumors began to surface, and a lot of "he said, she said" began to not only tear our marriage further apart, but it began to damage other relationships that were attached to us. One rumor that had surfaced that really bothered me was I being accused of having an affair with another minister. The questions were being fed as a family member or two questioned my husband as to why this person was around me all the time. Remember, we were all members of the same church. I assume that some were not accustomed to two ministers who attended the same church and were of opposite sex being able to have a platonic relationship. Once that small seed entered my husband's mind, it caused more division between us. Instead of asking me the question concerning my minister friend, they asked Vincent, and out of his emotions, he added fuel to the fire by entertaining the rumor. Vincent began responding out of his emotions and anger, and it began to cut off any open lines of communication between the two of us.

The lesson I learned concerning boundaries with this incident was to always fight to keep the lines of communication open between the two of us. When Vincent first brought the accusation to me, I immediately shut down in my spirit. I became very angry towards those family members and him. I was even more insulted and hurt by the fact that Vincent believed the rumor. Granted, we were on our way towards a divorce, but my integrity was being questioned by a person who I thought should know my character better than anyone. Shutting down was not the answer, yet it was my reaction to the rumor. Communication is not merely an option in marriage. If you want your marriage to survive, communication is critical! Hard circumstances will come, but you must find a way to express your feelings to your mate and allow him or her that same respect as well.

Women, most of us are natural communicators while men are usually the total opposite. We love to express, to talk, and to engage. In that moment when the rumor was brought to me, I needed some down time to gather my thoughts because I knew that if I had addressed it with our family members who were spreading it, I would have been very ungodly! I took the high road and took time to pray and ask God to help my heart and my mouth because I knew we would have to continue interacting even if it was just church business.

Another lesson that I picked up from this incident was to keep people on a need-to-know basis. This is an important boundary to set for your marriage as well. Family and friends mean well (hopefully), but they all come with their own personal biases. Once you expose what is going on in public, it will never be private again. Once Vincent decided to hold on to the rumor and repeat it to others, it caused those family and friends to form opinions of me and our marriage. In addition to that, it became a doorway for Vincent to have an open ranting session about how he might have felt in that moment. These scenarios expose your relationship to unnecessary scandal and also betray your mate. To prevent this from happening, we must be careful not to get in the habit of conversing about our spouse when we are influenced by negative emotions. Learn to keep the conversation light. The old saying that my grandmother taught me has been helpful: if you don't have anything positive to say, then be quiet!

Most times, in such situations involving gossip, the couple has moved past their arguments or problems that may have occurred prior to the spread of the rumor, but their social circle continues whispering about their past and has formed negative feelings towards one's mate and one's marriage. Managing your marriage by a committee (your family and friends' opinions) because you shared personal information that you shouldn't have can be detrimental. It can cause the premature death of your marriage. I don't know Malcolm X's in-laws, but this is what he had to say in a quote from his *Autobiography of Malcom X*, "My feeling about in-laws was that they were outlaws."

Malcolm either had this mindset going into his marriage, or he discovered it during. But I believe one thing is for sure: he believed in boundaries.

In an article by author Briana Ford, she mentions a Social Sharing Policy that couples should have when creating boundaries in their marriage. In her article, she recommends that couples have these discussions prior to marriage as to what will and will not be shared about their private lives. Sharing your love and testimonies or just beautiful pictures about your relationship can be encouraging to others, but this type of info can also be overshared. As a team, you both should agree with the "do's and don'ts" so that you are not violating each other's personal space as well as opening the doors to extra ridicule. It is undeniable that we live in a social media crazed world where everything is about how many likes we can get on our posts. Many have sacrificed their marriage to become socially popular. Although this was not a major issue with Vincent and me, I decided to offer my opinions regarding this issue in hopes that they may bring attention to an area you may have overlooked. Tweeting, posting, going live, snapchatting, etc. negatively about your marital status and or issues is a major "no-no" in my opinion. Some even go and change their marital status to things like, "it's complicated," which knocks down the fence to their privacy.

During our separation, I never changed my marital status simply because I didn't need the extra judgement that my marriage was failing. I also tried very hard not to post negatively about bad marriages and or bad husbands, although I may have had my own thoughts about those things in that season. Everyone who knew me had known me to be very positive on my pages, but there was this one time in which I had a short lapse of memory and decided to lash out in frustration about some things that were going on at the church concerning the way I felt I was being attacked. I am so thankful that my sister in ministry, "The Bombshell General" is what I call her, picked up the phone after I posted and told me to take it down. I was floored at the nerve of her telling me I was posting out of my emotions and that that wasn't how God wanted me to handle my issue. She further worked my nerves by telling me that my emotions would cause me to be off because I was going through my marital issues and that I was frustrated, and it was showing. Honestly, I knew she was right, but I was livid. I did take the post down, but I made a deal with myself that I would never post on social media when I was angry because it reminded me of a snake spewing out venom. Venom is destructive, and I didn't want to add that to what I was already dealing with in my heart towards my marriage.

At the end of the day, I appreciated my sister giving me that correction, which leads to my last lesson in this chapter: choose wisely. In telling you to choose wisely, I'm referring to the counsel or advice you seek for help with your marriage. I realize that marriages go through serious issues, and sometimes as a couple, we need to open that fence up and let someone else in to help. Third parties don't necessarily solve the problems in your marriage, but they can send you in the right direction towards a solution. Although I had many great preachers in my life, I wasn't comfortable with talking to everyone about our separation and the issues that led to divorce papers being signed. Wise men heed counsel of many advisors bearing fruit. Remember the fruit of a person's life is important. Is their marriage successful? How do they respond to their spouse? Are they professionals in this area? These are just a few questions you should ask before opening up to someone. I realize we all love to vent, but misery does like company, so even with that you must be careful. I would advise you to get individual counseling first and then maybe work your way up to the both of you getting counseling if your spouse agrees.

Remember, your marriage is sacred, and your responsibility is to keep intruders OUT while having the balance to allow the right team of people in. Just like no man is an island, the truth is no marriage is either.
Please be sure to pray first along with seeking the Word of God for your inner circle. I have listed below some of my favorite Scriptures to help you see that even God agrees with wise counsel.

Proverbs 12:15 ESV

The way of a fool is right in his own eyes, but a wise man listens to advice.

Proverbs 11:14 ESV

Where there is no guidance, a people falls, but in an abundance of counselors there is safety.

Proverbs 15:22 ESV

Without counsel plans fail, but with many advisers they succeed.

Proverbs 19:20-21 ESV

Listen to advice and accept instruction, that you may gain wisdom in the future. Many are the plans in the mind of a man, but it is the purpose of the LORD that will stand.

Lessons Learned

1. **Boundaries in your marriage are your responsibility. It is the couple's job to come together to make them for their relationship and to enforce them when it comes to others outside of their covenant, including family and friends.**

2. **Always be willing to fight to keep the lines of communication open between you and your spouse.**

3. **Choose wisely. At some point, all marriages will need counsel—just be sure yours is WISE.**

8

DIVORCE IS AN OPTION

I believe it's safe to say that when we decide to marry, our intention is forever and always. I believe that as part of the Christian community, we value the words of our vows as we stand before our significant others in front of at least one or two witnesses, and especially in the sight of God. I believe that our hearts have pure motives toward a bright future as we begin our new lives after we say I DO! Many feel so strong about it that we even have quotes like, "When I get married, it will be for life." One of the more popular ones that I've ran across and heard so many times is, "Divorce is NOT an option!" Well there are many of us who ended with a different result than these words and these quotes were not true in our case.

The truth of the matter is that DIVORCE IS AN OPTION! Not only is divorce just an option, but it is one that has been chosen countless times, especially in the Christian community. For many, divorce looked like the better choice than staying in a marriage in which they were unhappy or had issues that may have seemed unsolvable. Let me be very clear in my stance before we go any further. I do believe, and it is my hope and prayer, that once a couple is married, they honor those vows to each other and God, that they would make every effort possible to try to salvage and come to a resolve in their relationship. However, I am also aware that circumstances do exist in which the two parties are unable to work things out, and divorce is the result.

Every area of life has been addressed in the Bible, and divorce was definitely discussed in both the Old Testament and New Testament. When a subject is brought up in both testaments, I tend to feel as though God wanted to be sure He was heard and understood. The Bible is very direct with showing that God has seen marriage as a lifetime commitment between a male and female since the time it was instituted. In Malachi 2, God addresses the unfaithfulness of His people and the covenant that He made with them. God himself begins to address what He sees as treacherous behavior in the family unit, and He has some strong views on divorce! Let's take a look at Malachi 2:13-17 in the Amplified version:

13 This is another thing you do: you cover the altar of the LORD with tears, with [your own] weeping and sighing, because the LORD no longer regards your offering or accepts it with favor from your hand. 14 But you say, "Why [does He reject it]?" Because the LORD has been a witness between you and the wife of your youth, against whom you have dealt treacherously. Yet she is your marriage companion and the wife of your covenant [made by your vows]. 15 But not one has done so who has a remnant of the Spirit. And what did that one do while seeking a godly offspring? Take heed then to your spirit, and let no one deal treacherously against the wife of your youth. ¹⁶ *"For I hate* [a]*divorce," says the LORD, the God of Israel, "and him who covers his garment with wrong and violence," says the LORD of hosts. "Therefore keep watch on your spirit, so that you do not deal treacherously [with your wife]."*

¹⁷ *You have wearied the LORD with your words. But you say, "In what way have we wearied Him?" In that you say, "Everyone who does evil is good in the sight of the LORD, and He delights in them," or [by asking], "Where is the God of justice?*

Yes, right there in verse 16, God says, "I hate divorce." Hate is a very strong word, and there is no question to us as believers that divorce is not an option He desired for our lives. The word "hate" is an intense dislike for something. God despised it and addressed it with His people. I personally believe in my heart that there are many reasons why God felt so strongly about divorce. Let me share a few with you from my personal experience as a divorcee.

First, divorce is not a solution, but it is an exchange of problems. Most feel that once they get a divorce from their spouse, their world will automatically become better and their problems will be solved, but that is not the case. Typically, there is an exchange of pain. There is always loss associated with divorce. I've even used the word "death" as it related to my first divorce. All those years of sharing space with that mate—dead. All

95

the happy memories that were created—dead. Even some of the friends we both shared, those relationships died due to the divorce. I felt as if I had exchanged the anger towards being unhappy in the marriage for the grief that I was feeling as I looked at all the loss that the divorce had caused. God knew that the pain of a divorce would be horrendous for everyone involved, and I believe His stance was to keep us from experiencing those pains unnecessarily!

Secondly, divorce destroys the reputation of God's first institution. I've stated this before but will repeat it: before God created church, He created this organism of marriage to demonstrate covenant in the earth. Marriage was meant to be a special covenant between a man, a woman, and their God. It is the one relationship where God binds us together in the spirit, as one unit. When divorce takes place, it causes what God has bound together in the spirit to be ripped apart. Satan, God's enemy, our enemy, loves division, and divorce is just that, the dividing of a covenant that was made.

Marriages were created to glorify God in the earth so that a world that is desperate would see His love and His image through the closest relationship He designed. Divorce contradicts God's effort to show how we should operate towards one another as we are created in His image and likeness.

Not only does the divorce affect the two individuals, but the bystanders who are often innocent become traumatized. I'm speaking specifically about the children involved. Many times, they are not considered until the papers are signed and the guardian, parent, or a third party suddenly notices signs and symptoms of the pain they are experiencing. Feelings can range from insecurity, aggressiveness, anxiety, depression, low self-esteem, and anger, and can even become as extreme as suicide. Both parents must realize that children have feelings and opinions to what they see taking place. Keep in mind that God's original plan for our homes was to be a place where our children are to be nurtured. Our homes are where they learn character, values, integrity, and how to treat others. I'm not stating that this cannot and is not being done well in single parent households after divorce because I know it is. But let's stick to the subject of God's original purposes for marriage because God never suggested divorced. Divorce hurts. It destroys and offers no apologies for it.

As a divorcee, I recognize that there are reasons why people simply want out of their marriages. Abuse, particularly physical harm being forced on another, and adultery, especially on repeated accounts, are two of the main factors that have destroyed the marriages of couples I have coached. Some decided to work things out through more extensive counseling while others decided they couldn't take it anymore.

As I reflect on the divorce papers Vincent and I had to face, his reason for filing was neither of these; it was because of irreconcilable differences! As a culture, we have grown very familiar with this term concerning marriages or the excuse for ending them. This term is simply, in my words, a "no-fault clause" for the divorce. It means that neither party is more at fault for the marriage ending, and neither party wants to fix it—the marriage is unworkable. Couples just like us have decided that they don't want to work their issues out, so they want to go their separate ways and start over. I'm not heartless towards those who are unhappy in their marriages, but the enemy has us filled with so much pride and arrogance that if things don't go our way, we want OUT!

Obviously, this request for divorce was getting out of hand, so Jesus once again addressed the subject in New Testament. God had already spoken concerning His hate for divorce in the Old Testament, but the people wanted a way out, so Moses granted it. Let's see what the book of Matthew reads:

19 Now when Jesus had finished saying these things, He left Galilee and went into the part of Judea that is beyond the Jordan; ² and large crowds followed Him, and He healed them there.

³ And Pharisees came to Jesus, testing Him and asking, "Is it lawful for a man to divorce his wife for just any reason?" ⁴ He replied, "Have you never read that He who created them from the beginning MADE THEM MALE AND FEMALE, ⁵ and said, 'FOR THIS REASON A MAN SHALL LEAVE HIS FATHER AND MOTHER AND SHALL BE JOINED INSEPARABLY TO HIS WIFE, AND THE TWO SHALL BECOME ONE FLESH'? ⁶ So they are no longer two, but one flesh. Therefore, what God has joined together, let no one separate." ⁷ The Pharisees said to Him, "Why then did Moses command us to GIVE

HER A CERTIFICATE OF DIVORCE AND SEND HER AWAY?" [8] *He*

them, "Because your hearts were hard and stubborn Moses permitted you to divorce your wives; but from the beginning it has not been this way. [9] *I say to you, whoever divorces his wife, except for sexual immorality, and marries another woman commits adultery."*

[10] *The disciples said to Jesus, "If the relationship of a man with his wife is like this, it is better not to marry." Matthew 19:1-10 (AMP)*

Most of us know that the Pharisees hated Jesus and always wanted to twist his words concerning the law that had been written according to the words of God. They wanted to convince people that Jesus was contrary to God and wasn't the Savior they were looking for. Their tactics never worked, but that didn't stop them from trying. They waited until there was a crowd and began to test Jesus on the subject of divorce.

Jesus not only reminds the Pharisees that God hates divorce and doesn't take pleasure in it, but he tells them the reasons that He accepts as grounds for it. God states that Sexual Immorality is a reason for a divorce. Sexual Immorality is inclusive of fornication, prostitution, and/or adultery. These acts invade and cause division, both spiritually and physically, in marriage relations because God sees the two as one flesh! Imagine cutting something in half. It is now split, separated from the closeness of the other part of what was once joined together. Fornication was included because of Jewish custom. Once a couple was engaged, they were considered married. So, if immorality took place before that marriage was consummated, it was still grounds for divorce. Being unfaithful in a marriage doesn't mean that divorce is the requirement to solve the issue, but it is an allowance for the divorce from the guilty party. Ultimately, the resolution or work towards it is the couple's choice.

God's standard or stance on divorce never changed; however, He also gave leaders wisdom to make decisions based on what they experienced with the people. Therefore, Moses allowed divorce to settle relationships in which couples no longer desired to be together. Now keep in mind that only the male was granted the right to divorce his wife. Therefore, the Scripture says that a certificate of divorce had to be given to the woman. Otherwise, the divorce was not legal. Jesus is now reminding these religious leaders that Moses granted the divorces because of the hardness of men's hearts. Wow! Here come the irreconcilable differences! Those exceptions that man has come up with to justify the dissolution of the nuptials.

As Christians, we must be careful not to allow the spirit of divorce to hover over our marriages. Biblically, this may not be a proper term, but I am a firm believer that everything starts in the spirit realm and enters into the natural, which is the manifestation. If divorce can be manifested in the earthly realm, then it came from somewhere. Moses said it's the hardness of our hearts that caused men to desire divorce, so now we must be on alert to ensure protection of what God joined together.

⁸ Control yourselves and be careful! The devil is your enemy, and he goes around like a roaring lion looking for someone to attack and eat. 1 Peter 5:8 ERV (Easy2Read Version)

This passage is just a reminder that we have an enemy who desires to destroy us and our family unit. We must be watchful to not allow our hearts to harden in our marriages that will cause us to call it quits. We must be aware of what's happening in our marriages and be willing to provide a maintenance plan for the proper upkeep. I look at it like this: my car will not function properly or at its best if I don't take it for routine oil changes, rotation of tires, and basic cleaning. This is the same vehicle that I acquired when I went to a car lot and purchased it. Then I drove it off the lot with the intentions of taking good care of it so that it would function for a very long time. But if I fail to take care of it, I will end up stranded on the side of the road, or worst-case scenario, the car will break down to the point where it is no longer functional.

This is likened to our marriages. We must take care of the maintenance or our marriages will become dysfunctional as well. Listed below are a list of marital dysfunctions that I found in a great book that helped Vincent and me during this difficult time. Part of maintenance is to know what's needed, but it also includes the ability to tell when something is going wrong.

Seven Types of Dysfunctional Marriages

1.The Punctuators

These are marriages in which one or both spouses always "add up the dots" of the other spouse's behavior and then use that information to manipulate or control aspects of the marriage. Forgiveness is never really sought or truly given. Markers are always alert because they see marriage as a contest to be won against their spouse instead of something to be won in partnership.

2. The Fantasies

These couples have almost given up on pursuing a passionate intimacy with each other, so they often escape into fantasy through romance or pornography. The deeper you seek for fantasy, the more insensitive you become to real love and the more dissatisfied you feel with your spouse, your sex life, and your marriage.

3.Outsourcers

These dysfunctional couples "outsource" the most sacred aspects of marriage, which are emotional support, friendship, acceptance, companionship, and sometimes even sex, to other people or activities. They can also hurt their careers or give up their hobbies if they find fulfillment in these areas. They give their best to other people or activities at the expense of their marriage.

4. The Accusers

These are marriages in which one or both spouses always blame the other for all the problems of the relationship. These couples tend to have regular (often warm) discussions with no real solutions. Even when they are not arguing, their communication still contains a great deal of sarcasm and is annoying. They live in perpetual frustration with one another.

5. Individualists

These are couples who never seem to fully understand the partnership required for a healthy marriage. They live as two separate people with separate hopes, separate dreams, separate money, often separate bank accounts, separate hobbies, separate friends, and eventually separate lives altogether.

6. The Deceivers

These couples have no confidence in each other, and their lack of trust is perpetuated by keeping secrets and hiding details or hiding money, conversations, etc. from one another. Without trust and transparency in marriage, couples live in a state of artificial harmony and never experience true intimacy because secrecy is an enemy of intimacy.

7. Dropouts

These couples play with the word "divorce" in almost every disagreement until they finally go ahead and give

up on the marriage. They see the difficulties in marriage as an excuse to leave instead of an opportunity to work together and strengthen. They often remarry with another person and then repeat the same cycles of dysfunction   in   the   new relationship.
(The Seven Laws of Love by Davis Willis)

I wanted you as my reader to see these so that, hopefully, divorce doesn't have to be your portion, although it is an option. I hope to encourage you to understand that your marriage can be repairable and that there may be a maintenance plan that you can implement in order to help avoid divorce as an end result. I realize I don't have all the details of what has gone on or what is even currently happening, but I do know that there is nothing impossible with God's help.

I was encouraged when looking at several statistics on the divorce rate. An interesting fact is those who attend church on a regular basis are less likely to divorce than those who simply identify themselves as Christians. While a larger number of born-again Christians marry (84 percent) compared to the national average (78 percent), contemporary trends indicate that Americans are growing more comfortable with divorce. In its latest study, The Barna Group found that born-again Christians who are not evangelical are indistinguishable from the national average on the matter of divorce with 33 percent having married and divorced at least once. The research group noted that among all born again Christians, which includes evangelicals, the divorce figure is 32 percent, which is statistically identical to the 33 percent figure among non-born-again adults.

"There no longer seems to be much of a stigma attached to divorce; it is now seen as an unavoidable rite of passage," George Barna, who directed the study, stated in the study. (Source: The Barna Group, Ventura, CA)

I also found in my research that Professor Bradley Wright, a sociologist at the University of Connecticut, explains from his analysis of people who identify as Christians but rarely attend church, that 60 percent of these have been divorced. Of those who attend church regularly, 38 percent have been divorced. (Bradley R.E. Wright, *Christians Are Hate-Filled Hypocrites ... and Other Lies You've Been Told*, (Minneapolis, MN: Bethany House, 2010), p. 133.

My purpose in presenting these facts is to show that there is a difference in the numbers seemingly showing that although divorce is a choice, many who profess to be Christians are deciding to not elect that option. I would like to believe that it's because we are aligning ourselves with God's perfect will for our marriages, and that is to stay together. This is not to condemn anyone who has been divorced or who is going through one now. I know that circumstances can be out of our control, and marriage can be hard. My plea is that you will do all you can within yourself to save your marriage.

Vincent's and my paperwork had been turned in. According to Georgia law, our divorce should have been granted within 30 days, but God blocked it. Actually, when we were trying to figure out what was happening, we found out that several of our documents had been lost. True story! At that point, we decided that maybe irreconcilable differences were an excuse to not do our best to fix our relationship and that our pride had been in charge for too long. We took that as a sign that maybe we should try to fix our marriage rather than settle for divorce as our final decision.

Lessons Learned:

1. **Divorce is not a solution, but an exchange of problems.**

2. **Divorce destroys or hinders God's reputation of His first created institution, "Marriage."**

3. **God never approved of nor implemented divorce. He hates it. However, Moses instituted it because of the hardness of mankind's heart.**

9
RECOVERY IS A CHOICE

"RECOVERY in YOUR marriage is a process that
requires the attention of EVERYTHING you both
have left after the storm!"~SpeakO

I've come to realize that every storm in life is not meant
to destroy you but some are there to clear your path.
Storms are messy and often destructive, leaving behind
residue of their works. Storms are considered violent
disturbances of an atmosphere, a tumultuous reaction,
a controversy, an uproar to whatever is in their path.
Storms, even when referring to them in their natural
state, usually eliminate that which is not healthy in the
land according to nature. They still have an effect on
the portion that is healthy, but the storm can't destroy
it.

Usually what's left standing or functioning after a
hurricane, tornado, or snowstorm, etc. are the healthy
parts of nature that can be used to restart. After
deciding to try again in our marriage, that's what
Vincent and I had to decide on, restarting with the
healthy parts. We both knew that restarting would be

hard enough and that we both had to be fully invested in the process. I am so tickled and in tears because I reflect on the moment in which we reached that decision.

It's hilarious how, even with all the negative that was going on with the breaking of our marriage, we never lost contact. As a matter of fact, Vincent would show up at the house I was renting to cut my grass. He did it without my permission and without me even asking. We also texted and/or emailed often, even if it was just to fuss at each other. After finding out the divorce papers hadn't been processed, Vincent asked me to drop by his home to talk. Of course, I had to give him a tough time, but I went.

That night, we talked for hours. I was quite impressed that he cooked (considering Vincent hardly ever cooks) and had my favorite desert ready! Strawberries, pineapples, whipped cream, and chocolate. I knew this was a set-up, but I willingly walked right into it. If I had a wink button, I could put it on this page. It would go right here! Seriously, we both had a meltdown, which included very open and honest communication. For the first time in over a year, we were listening to each other to hear, not just to respond! We both waited for the other to get their thoughts across, and sometimes, there were moments when no response was needed. We realized that much of our issue had been broken communication. The entire time, we had been fighting because neither of us had listened properly. During this conversation, we knew that we wanted to recover our marriage, and from that night, we began executing certain principles that we both agreed would help.

Of course, communicating better was at the top of the list. Becoming an active listener was important. Not only listening to the words of your spouse, but reading his or her body language and facial expressions helps you to determine how he or she is feeling in that moment. As a female, we tend to use the words "fine" or "great" when that's not how we are truly feeling about something. A husband who is being an active listener can pick up on that and help his wife express herself simply because she sees he's really interested in what's wrong. Men, on the other hand, may be a little more complex because they tend to hold on to issues or deal with them internally. As a wife, we must learn how to provide a safe environment for them to speak freely. Ladies, try not to have an opinion about everything, or at least, don't voice it right away. Just let him talk and remember without interruptions.

Recovery demands forgiveness from you both. Unforgiveness is an unhealthy root that can destroy your marriage. Couples, we must purpose to forgive each other. Forgiveness requires truth to be out on the table, and many times, that truth may be uncomfortable. Vincent and I had to go back and reflect on the unpleasant subjects that made our marriage feel broken. We had to be open and honest with each other about conversations that we had with others, rumors that had circulated, and ex-spouses who tried to interfere during our break-up. None of these conversations were comfortable.

Forgiveness in your marriage is loving your mate enough to pursue healing instead of punishment when your mate has hurt you. We were needing to heal, and many days, it felt like being in a boxing match. This time, we were not each other's opponent, but fighting together to knock down obstacles that stood before us in that ring. Oftentimes, these rounds would appear to have us in separate corners, so we implemented what we call "PRACTICE THE PAUSE!" We have learned to pause when we're angry, pause when we're stressed, and pause when we're tired. The most important one is pausing to pray, especially before reacting to a situation. This keeps both parties from speaking negatively to each other in the heat of the moment. Of course, we won't always get this perfect, but it sure has helped!

Since this is a book concerning marriage, I want to plug in here: STOP DENYING YOUR SPOUSE SEX when you're angry! Let me be very candid. I would use sex as a weapon against my husband. This is another reason forgiveness is so important. In our recovery process, God has dealt with me on this issue because if I got angry with Vincent in the past, I would deny him. Sometimes, it would go on like this for weeks because I was a grudge holder. I always felt that sex was a reward for good behavior until the Holy Spirit directed me to these verses of Scripture.

Teaching on Marriage 1 Corinthians 7 (AMP)

7 Now as to the matters of which you wrote: It is good (beneficial, advantageous) for a man not to touch a woman [outside marriage]. ² But because of [the temptation to participate in] sexual immorality, let each man have his own wife, and let each woman have her own husband. ³ The husband must fulfill his [marital] duty to his wife [with good will and kindness], and likewise the wife to her husband. ⁴ The wife does not have [exclusive] authority over her own body, but the husband shares with her; and likewise, the husband does not have [exclusive] authority over his body, but the wife shares with him. ⁵ Do not deprive each other [of marital rights], except perhaps by mutual consent for a time, so that you may devote yourselves [unhindered] to prayer, but come together again so that Satan will not tempt you [to sin] because of your lack of self-control.

I was totally convicted after reading this. Actually, my heart sank because I realized that not only was I denying him of his benefits to my body as his wife, but I was unauthorized to do so. I was in direct violation of The Word of God! I quickly came to my senses and understood that even if I am upset, I don't have to be retaliatory. I realize there will be times where you both may not be on the same page, but learn to compromise in this area.

Of course, we want to govern ourselves according to the spiritual laws of God, but there are also both emotional and physical benefits connected to sex with our mates. In an article written by Sheri Stritof, entitled, "Why should you have sex more often," she explains the old adage "Just Do It" as it pertains to sex. She states that studies show increased emotional and physical benefits are tied to frequent sex with your spouse. Many of these listed I can vouch for.

Emotional Benefits of Having Sex

- Increases level of commitment
- Boosts self-esteem
- Makes a person feel younger
- Lowers the level of cortisol, a hormone that can trigger fatigue and cravings
- Lowers feelings of insecurity
- Keeps spouses connected emotionally
- Helps to give people a more positive attitude
- Makes a person more calm
- Makes a person less irritable
- Reduces depression
- Relieves stress

Physical Benefits of Having Sex

- Reduces risk of physical illness
- Improves immunity
- Reduces pain by increasing endorphins
- It's a form of exercise (it can help people achieve weight loss since about 200 calories are burned during 30 minutes of active sex
- Less-frequent colds and flu
- Vaginal tissue lubrication
- Lower mortality rates
- Reduced risk of prostate cancer

- Offers pain relief, including pain from migraines and back pain
- Improves posture
- Gives a youthful glow
- Reduces risk of heart disease
- Helps prevent yeast infections

- Lightens menstrual periods and cramps
- Firms stomach and buttocks
- Lowers blood pressure
- Helps people sleep better
- Improves digestion
- Improves sense of smell
- Has a therapeutic effect on immune system
- Better bladder control
- Healthier teeth
- Increased DHEA makes your skin healthier
- Improves fitness level
- Increases circulation
- Improves memory

After reading these, go ahead and do yourself a favor and indulge more in a gift that God created specifically for us married couples to enjoy. As you can see, it comes with benefits!

Our recovery needed Godly counsel. As a couple, I think it's wise to surround yourself with other couples that are influential to the direction in which your marriage is going. Our spiritual covering has been one of the most influential in our recovery process. We also have other couples that we often hang out with and fellowship with. It's good to see how other couples interact, and many times, you can share and get feedback with issues you may be dealing with in your relationship. We spoke with Momma Carol and Papa Nick each week, or as often as we needed, for them to encourage us and give us counsel. We even flew to Las Vegas as well as met up with them when they were in Georgia to spend quality couples time. Being around a couple that has been married for over 30 years and has endured some of the same issues proved to be inspiring for us. We both had to be willing and open to talk with them and implement principles and pointers to better our marriage. We knew they were praying for us and not judging our process. That made us even more relaxed around them. Both Vincent and I have lost our father's, so Papa Nick has also been a great father figure. There are times when just he and Vincent converse with each other, and I love that.

During our counseling with the Simpsons, they talked to us about dating each other on purpose. Sounds simple, but many couples have omitted that alone time with their spouses. We were one of those couples. We both work full-time jobs, we both serve in ministry in some capacity, and we have 5 children! There are always activities or something on the schedule to do! We now schedule alone time and date nights every week. We purpose to use this time just for us. Sometimes it's dinner and a movie, bowling, a sports event, and even pedicures together. Through this, we've become best friends because we are talking more and spending more time getting to know each other all over again. This may sound silly, but since we live on the East Coast and they live on West Coast, we all decided to post our date nights on social media. This is an opportunity for accountability in order to show we are being consistent, but it's also a way to encourage other couples to not forget about each other in this area. I believe in couple goals. Social media has been used as a tool to tear marriages apart, I believe in using it to build them up. I am encouraged to see what the

Simpsons are doing. There are even some weeks we suggested other couples to model them. Many of our social media friends have jumped on board, and it has become a positive way to share and encourage other couples to enjoy each other.

Prayer has become an essential part of our recovery also. Before, we had our separate prayer time, but now, we are praying together more often. Every morning before leaving the house, my husband is sure that we pray together. Even if it's just grabbing hands for less than three minutes, everyone under our roof is in a circle, heads bowed, and in prayer together. As a couple, we kneel at the feet of our bed at night and pray together. We are sure to pray for wisdom on how to continue to make our marriage pleasing to HIM and to one another.

Proverbs 24:3-4 says, *"By wisdom a house is built, and through understanding it is established; through knowledge its rooms are filled with rare and beautiful treasures." (NIV)*

I have learned to love to pray with my husband but also for him. In the past, my prayers for Vincent were centered around what I wanted and desired. God has begun to deal with my heart and help me to be mindful of my motives for my prayers. Instead of praying for Vincent because I wanted God to make him better for me, I now pray that God will make Vincent better for himself, and of course, for God's glory. I realize that if I pray this way, I am eliminating selfishness and pride while also trusting God to bring to pass His perfect will for my husband.

That leads to my next point in our process of recovery. We both are learning to focus on meeting each other's needs before our own. Whew! That hurt, I know! "Marriage is Ministry and Ministry is Serving. Don't get married if you don't want to serve!" In my Butterfly Boot Camp, this is a wisdom nugget I give to all my participants, especially those who are single. You can see their faces shift from smiling to a blank stare! I watch for their reaction because many have never heard anything like that, and it causes them to go into deep thought. Well, I can understand that response because when God spoke it to me, that was the same reaction I gave! Christian Missionary and Author, John C. Broger, stated this "Many conflicts in a marriage result from living to please self instead of living to please the Lord. These conflicts can be resolved and are actually opportunities for spiritual growth when dealt with in a biblical manner." That quote caused me to reflect on how I had been putting myself first and causing my own misery in most cases.

Even looking at that quote together made us realize that serving each other was God's way. The life of Christ is the best example of putting others before oneself as He laid His life down so that we may live. Every action Christ took was for the benefit of the other person, trusting that God would take care of Him. In your marriage, this doesn't mean that you neglect yourself; it means that you are willing to serve in your marriage God's way. Be sure to find balance in this area. If both of you are working hard to please each other, then how can happiness, peace, and joy not be present? Acts of serving in your marriage can involve a variety of gestures such as simply running your spouse's bath water, flirting with him or her more than usual (Vincent loves PDA), cooking his or her favorite meal, purchasing an unexpected gift, greeting him or her at the door after a grueling day at work, praying more for him or her than you do for yourself, or taking some of the load off his or her chore list (my hubby is great with this one). It's simply preferring your spouse's feelings, thoughts, or ideas, sometimes, before your own. Even giving them grace in an area where they may have messed up and deserved a different response is serving. It makes me feel so happy to see my husband smiling all the time because he is excited about our relationship again.

Learning to acknowledge and accept each other's differences is helping our healing as well. Acknowledging those differences wasn't our problem because we seemed to have mastered that part. We had become skilled at pointing out each other's problems without acknowledging our own as individuals. The problem was accepting those differences and not allowing them to become the mountain between us. We needed to understand our differences but also be willing to accept them and work together to become a better unit. Often, we expect our spouse to be exactly like us or operate the exact way we do. Keep in mind, your spouse comes from a different upbringing and sometimes culture as it pertains to his or her background. Both backgrounds collide in this one marriage. This integration of you two will likely have

117

some differences, so learn to be willing and open to accept them. You might discover, as my husband and I have, that the difference in your spouse is a strength that you need and vice versa!

Lastly, learning to work as a team has been beneficial for us. Instead of pulling each other in opposite directions in our marriage, we have learned that together we are stronger. Working together and purposely standing as a united front has allowed our household to become more peaceful. I feel more secure knowing that my husband and I are standing and fighting together. Working together helps you both to cover each other's weaknesses and reinforce each other's strengths. When one of us seems to stumble, the other one should be there to help. I was reading a story once about President Woodrow Wilson that inspired me concerning teamwork in a marriage. In the fall of 1919, President Wilson experienced a nervous breakdown and a cerebral hemorrhage that paralyzed his entire left side. His wife stepped in to protect him from the press and coordinated his executive responsibilities. She realized that her husband was incapable of performing his presidential duties, so she implemented a plan that would cover him. Those who wished to talk to the president had to go through Mrs. Wilson. It wasn't until years later that the public realized how ill the president had been and how Mrs. Wilson had helped her husband by doing all that he could not. She simply did what was necessary for her husband to finish his presidential term, and the president relied on his wife to keep everything running smoothly. They worked as a team. Never once was it mentioned that she shamed him for this disaster that happened in their lives, and he had to trust that she was capable of getting the job done. Teamwork in your marriage is about covering each other and not exposing one another.

In every boxing match, there's always two opponents. They are usually waiting on the bell to ring in order to start and/or stop the fight. Marriage will always have opposition because every good thing that God created was, has been, and will be attacked by an enemy. The goal is that we are on the same side of the ring with our spouse, ready to fight the real enemy and every attack launched by the devil. We must fight according to the principles of God, and we must do it together. My battle is still in progress, but I'm now on the winning side.

Lessons Learned:

1. **Recovery for your marriage is a choice, and both spouses must be willing to do the work.**

2. **Forgiveness in your marriage is loving your mate enough to pursue healing instead of punishment when they have hurt you.**

3. **Marriage is ministry and Ministry is SERVING each other!**

120

Really God?
Book Excerpt

In 2007, the overwhelming feeling of shock and grief exploded in my body because at this very time in my life, I felt my whole world had come crashing down all around me. This was the year my mentor, my best friend, yes, my father, had died. And if this had not been detrimental enough, several months later, my husband and I were kicked out of a church where we were leaders and had been serving for over five years, and to top the year off, we were going through a divorce of enormous proportions after eight years of marriage.

In fact, one day during this time, I can still recall vividly sitting alone on my living room floor, screaming (at the top of my lungs as loud as I could without choking) and crying streams of warm tears that simply dropped down my cheeks and onto the floor, leaving a small puddle. As I sat in my living room, one of my favorite rooms in the house, I realized the very room that used to bring me joy and was once filled with laughter had, in a twist of fate, become a room of mourning and sorrow and sadness. I sat there, feeling all alone with a sense of strange abandonment on one side, yet on the other, feeling the presence of God—only a small, still presence. In that moment of deep sorrow, I hung on to His presence as the tears kept flowing through my bloodshot eyes, gazing specifically towards my ceiling, and I let out a shout, "Really God!" a shout that sent a wave through my body and throughout my home. That shout should have been heard from miles away and must have reached through dimensions into the Holy of Holies. Nevertheless, I heard nothing from God but my own screams, and it seemed, at that very moment, God had abandoned me.

Quietly, I questioned myself, "How can all of this be happening to me?"

Then I questioned God, "Have I not done all you asked? Where are you in the midst of this mess?"

"What have I done so wrong that I deserve all of this at one time?"

Look, if you're honest with yourself, you have asked the same question or something very similar. "Really God?" I believe that every Christian or every person, at some point, will ask this question. We ask this question based on life's trials, tribulations, or unexpected things that go on in our lives. Disappointment, discouragement, and just different things that happen cause us to ask that question, *"Really God, am I really going through this for the first time, the second time, or the third time?"* As believers, it is possible we may have all asked this question to God at one time or another. Many of us may not be so eager to admit willingly that we have asked the question, "Really God?" or even, "Is this happening to me again?"

Whatever form we ask it in, I believe that many times in our lives, we are asking God based on what we're going through. "Why is this happening? Am I really going through this?" I believe that God placed this book in my spirit simply because I am a woman. Once, someone asked me to give them one word that best described me, and the word that came to my mind was *resilient*, so I want to be able to give a gift back to the Body of Christ to let them know that resilience really can be a gift that God gives us. If we look over our lives, we'll see that we have been able to bounce back from some things that we've been counted out of. In other words, we have been able to bounce back from many situations that we would not have thought we were able to come out of on our own.

As you read this book, let me just be honest. It is not for everyone!

This book is for the people who feel like they are in a dark place in their life right now.

This book is for that person who feels trapped in a situation and can't see a way out.

This book is for the people who feel like they have had enough and are saying, "If one more thing happens, I'm going to lose it!"

This book is for that person who is holding on to the promise of God but just can't see how it will happen, yet!

This book is for the people who know in their heart there has to be a way out but just don't know how to get there!

This book is bound to inspire, motivate, and help coach you out of your problem, through your process, and into your promise.

For every setback, God has your BOUNCE BACK in mind.

Order Your Book Today

About the Author

Orienthia Renee Speakman is tagged by many as "The Keep It Real Preacher"! Her energetic and transparent messages have touched the hearts of individuals both near and abroad. Her ability to take biblical principles and teach others how to use them in a practical way has been what has drawn much attention to her in recent years.

She has been ordained in ministry since October 2000. She has effectively served in various compacities, as her heart is to operate with excellence in whatever role she is in. A college graduate with a BS in Psychology, she currently serves her local church as the Christian Education Pastor. Orienthia's love for education has her in pursuit of ultimately earning a Doctorate in Ministry.

Orienthia can minister on many topics but her heart is for helping others to renew, rebuild and reinvent themselves after tragedy. Orienthia often says, "Every individual has the right to have a strong comeback from any setback in their lives. There is power in their process and my goal is to help them to be committed to their RESILIENCE!"

Her ministry and business Speak O Worldwide houses a variety of resources to nurture broken individuals into wholeness. Her Butterfly boot camp was created specifically for the needs of women who has been divorced, widowed or just making bad choices in relationships and desire to be healed. It is a 9- week course that can be done from home via telephone or internet. Her coaching services, books and other materials can also be found on her website.

Orienthia loves speaking, writing, and being a Transformation Coach, but her priority is her marriage! Her book *"Marriage Vs. Ministry, The Fight of My Life"* is a candid, uncensored tool to share the dangers of an improper balance between the two. She and her husband Vincent were almost another statistic for divorce but used the principles in this book to not only save their marriage but to have a healthy one. This couple share 5 beautiful children and reside in Stone Mountain, Georgia.

Contact Information: www.speakorienthia.com
Fb Contacts: Orienthia Speakman
              Speak O
              Butterfly University IG
Contact: pastorospeaks

www.ingramcontent.com/pod-product-compliance
Lightning Source LLC
LaVergne TN
LVHW052031080426
835513LV00018B/2280